THE

Distributed by:

Australia
Christian Press,
3 Harley Crescent,
Condell Park 2200,
Sydney,
Australia.

New Zealand
Gospel Publishing House Society Ltd.,
154 King Street,
PO Box 74,
Palmerston North,
New Zealand.

Singapore
Scripture Union Distributors,
413 Tagore Avenue,
Singapore 2678.

South Africa
Christian Art Wholesale,
20 Smuts Avenue,
Box 1599,
Vereeniging 1930,
South Africa.

THE WINNING CHURCH

CHURCH GROWTH EVANGELISM FOR TODAY!

ROLAND E. GRISWOLD

 Scripture Press

Amersham-on-the-Hill, Bucks HP6 6JQ, England

ISBN 0 946515 19 0

Scripture quotations in this book are from the *Holy Bible, New
International Version,* © 1973, 1978, 1984, International Bible
Society, published by Zondervan Bible Publishers. Other quotations
are from *The Living Bible* (TLB), © 1971 by Tyndale House Publishers;
the *Revised Standard Version* (RSV), ©1946, 1952, 1971, 1973; and
the *King James Version* (KJV). All quotations by permission of the
publishers.

Designed and printed in Great Britain for
SCRIPTURE PRESS FOUNDATION (UK) LTD
Raans Road, Amersham-on-the-Hill, Bucks HP6 6JQ by
Nuprint Ltd, Harpenden, Herts AL5 4SE.

CONTENTS

MY THANKS TO:

The Rev. David McCarthy of Aurora, Illinois,
who has been a helpful adviser,
and
Susan Gettis, who patiently typed the manuscript.

FOREWORD

Victory and Defeat are not concepts with which the local church in Britain feels comfortable. One smacks of glib triumphalism; the other of unacceptable admission. Yet both experiences are facts of life!

When relationships are being established within a church, numbers added to the congregation, an active contribution to the community is being made and the good news of the Gospel declared, then surely that church is winning! But so often we find the prospect of Victory and Defeat unwelcome and threatening.

Page upon page has been written in various attempts to encourage growth in the local church. My initial reaction to the appearance of Roland Griswold's book was to shudder at the prospect of yet more trans-Atlantic hypothesis for success in the British church. I was mistaken. The book avoids overbearing dogmatism and stridency in its tone. The author sums up his own purpose for the book in terms which he fulfils within its pages.

"The purpose of this book has been to expand your vision to see new possibilities for outreach through your church, to help you learn from methods used by early churches and Christians, and to intoduce principles and methods you might use to help make your congregation a more powerful force in reaching the lost of your community. "Make disciples," was the Master's command; we dare not busy ourselves with other tasks and leave this one undone."

It is surely not enough for us to content ourselves with the facile phraseology of Grantland Rice.

> For when the One Great Scorer comes
>   To write against your name,
> He marks—not that you won or lost—
> But how you played the game.

Just to have buried our talent in the ground is not an adequate response. Yet there are no easy answers. That which is helpful in one church may not work in another. A successful evangelistic method in one part of the country could fail dismally in another. What remains constant are the principles behind evangelism.

It is the principles expounded by Mr Griswold that are important, whether or not we adopt the practical hints and advice he offers. We must develop the principles in order that the local church may be seen as the foundation stone of evangelism.

Success must not be viewed from the perspective of a national map. It is within the local church that we face the acid test. And defeat is not acceptable!

CLIVE CALVER (B.D. Hons)
GENERAL SECRETARY
EVANGELICAL ALLIANCE

INTRODUCTION

World events provide daily reminders that the return of Christ is near. We do not know how much longer we have to challenge our generation with the Gospel. Christians are awakening to the opportunities before us to make disciples for Jesus Christ. Two symbols suggest our responsibility: the hook and the crook. A hook is used for catching fish, the picture of winning people for Christ. The shepherd uses a crook to guide sheep along the way. Our responsibility to our new converts is to lead them into mature Christian living and active membership in Christ's church.

Christ expects His church to grow. Dr. Win Arn, founder/director of the Institute for American Church Growth said in a recent letter to me, "Church expansion doesn't happen in general. It happens in specifics—as individual Christians and individual churches come alive to seeing the harvest around them, then praying that the Lord of the harvest will thrust forth labourers, identifying responsive people, focusing efforts, and persisting until God gives the increase." This book will help you and your church become involved in doing these five specifics.

Since January, 1979 I have served as Director of Church Expansion of the Advent Christian General Conference. My preparation began in 1955 when, through the instrumentality of the Rev. Milford Butterfield, I began my ministry as a home mission pastor in Orlando, Florida. In 1960 I developed a close relationship with the Rev. Hugh Shepard, then director of Home Missions. Under his guidance I developed the book and study material, *Analyzing Your Church and Community*. Then, in 1978, I did graduate work in Church Growth under Dr. C. Peter Wagner, professor at Fuller Theological Seminary. This study helped clarify the concepts that had developed in my mind regarding methods for fulfilling the Great Commission. So I pay tribute to these three whom God has used along with others to channel my thinking regarding the expansion of Christ's church.

Shakespeare wrote:

There is a tide in the affairs of men,
Which, when taken at the flood, leads men on to fortune;
Omitted, all the voyage of their life
Is bound in shallows and in miseries.
On such a full sea we are now afloat,
And we must take the current when it serves,
Or lose our ventures.

Julius Caesar, III.ii

The tide is at the flood for reaching people for Christ in our country. We have a ripe field, waiting for us to harvest it. As Shakespeare put it, "On such a full sea we are now afloat, And we must take the current when it serves, Or lose our ventures." This is the time for Christians, who love the second coming of Christ, to remember that it is the message of His first coming that saves men and women. Now is the time for taking the message of the kingdom to the hundreds of people around us who face certain destruction at His second coming if they do not receive Him as Saviour and Lord and become involved as responsible members of His church. Let's fulfill our commission by hook and crook.

1

Why all the talk about growth?

Why do some churches grow while others die?

Two letters in today's mail reminded me of the urgency which makes this book necessary. One letter is from a pastor of an old established church in an industrial city. The area population has been decreasing for many years. Yet the church is alive and well. The pastor, young and in his first pastorate, is convinced that he should use only methods that produce positive results. Result: an enthusiastic core of laypersons in the church, trained and motivated to become involved in worship, education, and evangelistic outreach to their city. Membership is rising rapidly. There are numerous baptisms, and attendance has increased 50 percent in the past two years.

The other letter came from a pastor who was expressing the frustration of having given the church his best and still it was dying. "Why is nothing happening in this congregation?" he asked. The church is in a good location in an expanding metropolis. Population in a three-mile radius has increased by 3,000 in the last two years, and 7,500 new residents are expected in the next three years. But unless God performs a miracle there, that church will be closed by the time you read this book.

More churches can identify with the second church than

with the first. Annual reports show two-thirds to three-fourths of our American congregations have not increased in membership in the past two years. Many have seen declines of 10 percent or more in that period, yet few of the churches are situated where there is no potential for growth. The North Pole and Death Valley represent two extremes where church expansion isn't likely to occur, and our research doesn't show a congregation in either spot.

Why do some churches grow while others die? Could it be that some churches are praying, planning, and working for an increase, while others are not? The letters to the seven churches in Asia Minor in Revelation 2 and 3, make it clear that Christ *expects* His churches to be growing. The Lord is awakening Christians to this reality. There is a new openness to the concept that an increase in numbers is not "unspiritual" or in opposition to maturing in quality.

Growth in quality results in growth in quantity; growth in quantity makes growth in quality possible. A church expands when the members grow in grace (quality). Part of that quality includes sharing Christ with people who repent, believe in Christ, are baptized, added to the church, and themselves begin maturing in grace. The cycle should be endless.

The parables of Matthew 25 have particular meaning for evangelical Christians. The Ten Virgins illustrates the need for alert preparation for Christ's second coming, whereas the Talents stresses the need for faithful service during His absence. "Occupy till I come" is the *King James* translation of the command in the similar Parable of the Pounds (Luke 19:11-27). The NIV makes it clear the reference is not just to occupying a seat in a building for two hours on Sunday: " 'Work,' He said, 'until I come back.' "

Why all the talk about growth? Because the Lord intends for His church to grow! Let's expand on this premise.

Bible Base
Read Matthew 28:19-20. Underline the verbs. The command verb is *make*. The other three are supporting verbs: going,

baptizing, teaching. Christ's marching orders to His church during the time between His ascension to heaven and His second coming is: *make disciples.* That commission has never been changed or withdrawn.

Going refers to our daily walk—at home, in the neighborhood, at work. Wherever we happen to be, we should *make disciples.*

Baptizing indicates that a person has been made a member of Christ's church and is part of a local fellowship of believers.

Teaching believers to obey requires developing in them an obedient will. It means each believer is committed to doing the will and work of God on a continuing basis.

Dr. Donald McGavran served for over forty years as a missionary in India. Upon returning home, he was appalled at the lack of growth among American churches. He began teaching the principles learned in India to promote growth here. He serves as Dean Emeritus of the School of World Mission at Fuller Theological Seminary, and is known as the father of the modern church growth movement. He states: "The congregation which is not engaged in proclaiming Christ to men and women, persuading them to become His disciples and responsible members of His church, may be a religious club, but it is not the body of Jesus Christ. His body is filled with His Spirit and engaged in finding lost men and women."[1]

With the Great Commission in sharper focus, the next Scripture passage illustrates how the Commission can be successfully carried out in your life and in your church. Read John 15:1-17.

Picture the relationship between the vine, the branches, and the fruit. Christ is the vine, we are the branches, and the fruit is the result of our faithful obedience to Christ's command. Christ emphasized the relationship several times. He reminds us that a branch is a branch . . . is a branch . . . is a branch. It is *not* the vine. (See vv. 1-2 and 6.) The branch is totally dependent on the vine for its life and strength.

"You did not choose Me, but I chose you to go and bear

fruit—fruit that will last" (v. 16). What fruit is borne by a person in vital union with Jesus Christ? In light of the Great Commission, the person is thoroughly involved in making disciples.

Commenting on verse 16—"I chose you to go and bear fruit"—Everett Harrison in *Wycliffe Bible Commentary* says: "Christ ordained them [the disciples] with service in mind.... Previously (vs. 9) the fruit meant love. Now it was to mean love in action, the heralding of the message of salvation and the winning of souls."[2]

Why all the talk about growth? Because Christ calls His people to expand the membership roll of the kingdom! New Testament evangelism is the primary task of every Christian and every church.

We Must Grow

Matthew 28:19-20 and John 15:1-17 point out the clear command of Christ to His church: "Be busy about the task of *making disciples.*" Persons who have heard the Gospel, have become Christ's disciples, and have become responsible members of His church are in a position to bear fruit. Disciples who have become part of a local fellowship and are continually being taught by the Scriptures, the Holy Spirit, and other Christians *will* bear fruit. The only way Christ's church can increase is for His children to go out and reach others. It is a continuing cycle: *finding* the lost; *folding* them into the church; and *fielding* them back into their world where they can begin *finding.*

Christ's church must not for a moment overlook the great social and physical needs in society. Yet simply illustrating the compassion of Christ is not enough. That reduces the church to just one more humanitarian agency rather than a movement to bring people into right relationship with God. My service for the Master must be a definite part of my church's strategy to reach our community for Christ or I'm out of step with the Great Commission.

An example of the kind of expansion that God expects is

seen in the Book of Acts, where the cycle moves at tremendous speed: 120 in the Upper Room; 3,000 more on the Day of Pentecost; and in just a few years Paul reported that tens of thousands of Jews alone had turned to Christ and become part of the church. Acts 19 and 20 describe the establishment of the churches in Asia Minor by Paul on his third missionary tour. It was indeed an exciting time. The area was ripe for the Gospel. Public debates, burning of the writings of false cults, and even a riot marked the impact of the Gospel on the whole area.

In *The Fervent Prayer*, J. Edwin Orr states: "The church began to spread by extraordinary praying and preaching... together with the irrepressible kind of personal witnessing.... The first three centuries of progress were followed by a millennium... rightly called the Dark Ages, though they were not entirely without light. Before the fifteenth century, a change began, commencing a progression of awakenings that moved the church by degrees back to the apostolic pattern and extended it all over the world."[3]

Dr. Orr then ably traces the rise of spiritual awakenings at irregular intervals over the past 600 years. He makes the significant point that this ebb and flow of obedience to the Great Commission has marked the church down through the centuries.

Are We Growing?

Since evangelism *is* God's will for His church, how does my church rate? Do I see joy and excitement in our congregation as new people regularly come to Christ? Is there evidence of spiritual vitality: people becoming serious students of Scripture, more effective in prayer, more open in witnessing to what Christ is doing in their lives, more faithful in stewardship of their finances, more regular in using their spiritual gifts?

Healthy churches have some identifying characteristics. Compare your church with this chart. On a scale of 1-5, rate your church, with 5 if your church is just like this and 1 if unlike this.

Four Basic Ministries of a Healthy Church

	Rating
Edification (primarily the Sunday service) —Christians eager for participation in worship, praise to God, instruction from the Word of God, praying together for one another and their world.	

Evangelism (finding and reaching pagans)
—At least 20 percent of the members regularly going out to find lost people in the community.
—Sharing Christ wherever they find pagans, rather than just inviting them to church.
—Continuing involvement with lost people until they receive Christ as Saviour and come into His church.

Fellowship (building up one another)
—Warm sharing with all members.
—Encouraging one another.
—Aware of Christ's presence in our midst when we are together.

Service
—Compassion for human needs in our community.
—Developing ministries to touch those needs.

In contrast, a diseased congregation would have very little meaningful activity in any of these areas. The members gather on Sunday like spectators, watching and hearing the pastor and choir. Rather than reaching out to lost neighbors, they say, "The pastor is trained; we pay him to win the lost in our community." There is little fellowship, at least in the New Testament sense. Members isolate themselves in little cliques, giving no picture of unity with others in the church. Service may be limited to taking an annual offering for world hunger, or paying someone else to do good deeds. No one gets personally involved in healing the hurts of society.

An increasing membership will cause some pleasant problems for your church. For example:

—You will face a continual need to train teachers for new Sunday School classes that are formed to serve the larger membership.

—You may have to plan double sessions for Sunday School and worship, or study plans for an addition or relocation so the increasingly larger congregation can receive adequate ministry.

—You might have a committee looking for locations for branch Sunday Schools and home Bible studies to reach the unsaved in the various neighborhoods where members live.

—You may consider establishing a mission in a new subdivision where some of your newer members live.

What types of ministries might help your church to put the Great Commission into shoe leather? Here are a few ideas. How many has your church tried in the past year? Circle either *yes* or *no*.

1. Community survey to locate unchurched families. Yes / No

2. Training course in personal evangelism. Yes / No

3. Regular lay visitation of the unchurched in the community. Yes / No

4. Regular prayer for specific lost persons. Yes / No

5. Outreach to non-Christians through small home meetings. Yes / No

6. Advertising our ministries to build community awareness. Yes / No

7. Personal weekly follow-up of those who visit a service. Yes / No

8. Families assigned to help new Christians become a real

21

part of the church family. Yes / No

9. Classes for new members at least twice a year. Yes / No

While these evangelism methods will not guarantee that your church will expand, omitting them may guarantee that your church will *not* grow.

Why all the talk about growth? Because Christ commanded it, the early church set a clear example, and we are living in a time when over 50 percent of the people in most areas do not know Jesus Christ as personal Saviour.

Remember Jesus' words; they are as fresh and true today as they were when He first phrased them: "If you obey My commands, you will remain in My love.... You are My friends if you do what I command.... I chose you to go and bear fruit.... Bear much fruit, showing yourselves to be My disciples.... Therefore go and make disciples."

By the end of this book, you are going to have many ideas to aid you in developing answers for your church. Each chapter will stimulate your thinking. Discuss your ideas with others who are reading this book. Then together with your pastor draw up some bold visionary plans for reaching the pagan population of your community. With God's guidance and strength, your church can be reaping a harvest for Christ in your community.

2

Be a nonconformist

'Nonconformists' are those who exercise spiritual
gifts for Christ's Kingdom.

Romans 12:1-8

¹Therefore, I urge you, brothers, in view of God's mercy, to offer your bodies as living sacrifices, holy and pleasing to God—which is your spiritual worship. ²Do not conform any longer to the pattern of this world, but be transformed by the renewing of your mind. Then you will be able to test and approve what God's will is—His good, pleasing, and perfect will.

³For by the grace given to me I say to every one of you: Do not think of yourself more highly than you ought, but rather think of yourself with sober judgment, in accordance with the measure of faith God has given you. ⁴Just as each of us has one body with many members, and these members do not all have the same function, ⁵so in Christ we who are many form one body, and each member belongs to all the others. ⁶We have different gifts, according to the grace given us. If a man's gift is prophesying, let him use it in proportion to his faith. ⁷If it is serving, let him serve; if it is teaching, let him teach; ⁸if it is encouraging, let him encourage; if it is contributing to the needs of others, let him give generously; if it is leadership, let him govern diligently; if it is showing mercy, let him do it cheerfully.

We are a three-car family. All three cars have over 100,000 miles on the odometers, and hardly a week goes by that I do not have to replace a worn part to keep one of them going. For years I used a stack of two-by-six boards for a ramp to elevate the cars for service. That was all right for a grease job or oil change; two boards under each front wheel raised the car sufficiently. But major repairs really presented a problem. It wasn't safe to drive the car up on more than two boards, so I dreaded working on the exhaust system or transmission.

Shortly before Christmas one year, the Pontiac reminded us loudly that it needed a new muffler. I bought one but couldn't get motivated to install it. Finally, the day before Christmas I got out the tools. But I couldn't get the car raised enough to replace the muffler. Just then my daughter Melodie came to me, insisting that I go with her for a last-minute shopping trip. Saved! That was all the excuse I needed to put off the dreaded task.

Only the next day did I realize my daughter purposely kept me from trying to replace that muffler on Christmas Eve. I unwrapped a pair of shiny metal car ramps as a Christmas present and saw the note, "To Dad with love, from Melodie." What a difference it made having the car securely raised on those ramps while I worked on it. And that gift has continued to make my repair tasks easier on the old cars ever since.

People who are not Christians have a missing part. Our Lord came that people might have His abundant life, but sin has separated us from that. The Great Commission is really a call for Christians to organize a massive campaign to install what is missing in people's lives. We have the needed missing part: new life through repentance of sin and faith in Jesus Christ as Lord and Saviour.

I thought of my experience with the car as I read the study, *Religion in America 1983-84,* prepared by the Princeton Religion Research Center. It seems that faithful church attendance and active service for Christ is the exception rather than the rule for many Americans. Christians seem to be missing something, just as I was missing those car ramps. A startling number of church members indicate they have never shared their faith with non-Christian men and women in their community. Many Christians are discovering that only one convert in five comes from outside the church. Perhaps we have been negligent in sharing our faith with our neighbors.

Must this be the norm for the church in the last days? Not if we believe Christ who said, "I will build My church, and the gates of hades will not overcome it" (Matt. 16:18). The parables He told about His kingdom all indicate growth. The Great Commission makes enlarging His church (kingdom) our primary concern and task. Christ does not expect the impossible of us. Nevertheless the question remains: If most Christians are not active in the business of making disciples, why should I be a nonconformist? Why should I have to swim upstream when everyone else is floating downstream with the current?

There are several reasons why you should not conform to the example of most Christians. For me the primary reason is that Christ has commanded us to make disciples. And there is also a selfish reason. You know the blessings that come if you are already involved in some way in making disciples in the community. There is a sense of joy and fulfillment when you see people coming to know Christ through the efforts of your church. An Air Force sergeant attended an Orlando, Florida church with his wife. He sensed the caring concern expressed by the members and began bringing other men with him from the air base. After a few months of hearing the Gospel preached and sensing the love of Christ in the church members as they witnessed to them, four of the airmen responded to an invitation to receive Christ on Easter Sunday. What a happy day! The members surrounded those men at the altar, with streams of joyful tears pouring down their cheeks. Soon there was a spontaneous singing of the doxology. You can be sure that that experience motivated the people to be even more faithful in their witness for Christ.

The Great Commission means that every Christian is to witness to what Christ is doing in his or her life.

Bible Base

Read Romans 12:1-8. Christians are members of a great body of believers. We are not isolated units of life but must function in relation to and interaction with the other members of our church. This is why most of Paul's letters are written to the local fellowship of believers rather than to individual Christians. Our involvement with other Christians in the work of making disciples is a necessary ingredient for success.

"Therefore ... in view of God's mercy" (v. 1). When the word *therefore* appears in Scripture, you should stop and see what it is *there for*. Paul is drawing a conclusion based on the facts in the first eleven chapters. "God's mercy" is Paul's way of describing the great acts of love God has shown to us. Those acts result in our redemption from sin and restoration as children of God. You and I are encouraged to give ourselves wholly to God as an act of worship in response to what He has done for us.

Earl Palmer, in *Salvation by Surprise,* comments on the phrase, "Do not conform any longer to the pattern of this world," when he says "These words amount to a dare to the Christian to challenge the right of the present age to ... impress its shape upon the Christian life."[1] Why should I be a

27

nonconformist? So I can test and approve what God's will is for me. Paul assures us that God's will is good, acceptable, and complete. Christians in Rome and in your church can refuse to accept the world's agenda for life. We cannot escape the pressures of the age, but we can let God make the entries in our appointment book of life. Then Romans 11:36 gives meaning to life: "For from Him and through Him and to Him are all things." That's completeness—past, present, and future.

How does a life of nonconformity to the world operate? Verses 3-5 say our relationship with God and fellow Christians is one of humility and unity. I don't have to deceive others by phrases that suggest false humility. Nor do I have to fear being judged by others if I do not match up to some human standard of perfection. There is no need to play games with God, with others, or with myself.

After urging us to have a sober view of our spiritual maturity, Paul teaches about spiritual gifts. How would you describe the relationship of the members of your church with each other? Verses 4 and 5 compare the church to a healthy body. My hands hold a hymnbook; my eyes see the notes and words; my brain sends impulses to my larynx and mouth; my ears hear the resulting sound as I sing. My ability to function would be greatly impaired if I had three mouths and no ears, or four hands and no eyes. Just so, the church functions properly only when each member does what God has called and gifted him or her to do. God places in each congregation persons with the necessary gifts for that church to function properly.

Verses 6-8 describe some of the spiritual gifts and how they function in a healthy church. Look at the passage and circle the seven gifts. The Princeton Religion Research Center survey seems to say that we are living in an era when many Christians are of the sit-and-soak variety. Those who exercise their spiritual gifts to extend Christ's kingdom are nonconformists. The word translated gifts in verse 6 is *charismata* in Greek, and the word grace is *charis*. Note an interesting progression: In verse 1 Paul encourages us to give our total selves to God as a gift. Then our gracious God in response gives spiritual gifts to us. We have freedom to use these gifts within the church to bring glory to Him and spiritual growth to ourselves and others.

God gives different gifts to each of us. Not every Christian is gifted to preach, to teach, or heal the sick, or lead people to Christ, or provide hospitality. But within our church there is a rich variety of gifts. Together we can carry out all the programs needed to find the pagans in our community, and provide that missing part by bringing them to saving faith in Jesus Christ and helping them to become responsible members. C. Peter Wagner, in *Your Spiritual Gifts Can Help Your Church Grow,* lists three benefits of knowing about spiritual gifts: You will be a better Christian and more able to allow God to make your life count for Him; they help you as an individual Christian and the church as a whole; and God is glorified as we use our gifts.

Romans 12:6-8 lists seven gifts that might affect the expansion of your church. Here is the basic definition of spiritual gifts:

> A spiritual gift is a special attribute given by the Holy Spirit to every Christian according to God's grace for use within the church.

It equips the Christian for the work of service and ministry.

Implication
To help in understanding these gifts, how they work, and which spiritual gifts you may have, we will define and describe them.

Prophecy is the special ability God gives some Christians to receive and communicate an immediate message of God with authority. We tend to equate prophecy with predictions of the future. Sometimes this is the case, but in biblical usage it was more often a word for the present. The basic meaning of the word *prophecy* is to speak forth, or to speak for another. The gift of prophecy is the ability to speak for God. Prophecy is also translated "preaching" and "inspired utterance." Often pastors and teachers have been chosen because they have this gift. As they use it, persons learn of Christ and how to become His followers.

Service (or ministry) is the gift that enables some Christians to see the unmet needs in the lives of members of the congregation and use the resources at hand to meet those needs. The word in Greek is our word for deacon.

Teaching is the God-given ability to communicate spiritual truth in such a way that the hearers learn. It is similar to preaching. Teaching places primary emphasis on instruction and guidance, while preaching seeks out action based on what has been learned. Teaching about sin and Christ's cure is vital to help people become Christians.

Encouraging is the ability to comfort, counsel, console, encourage, and exhort other members of the congregation as they live and minister. Consider Barnabas, whose name means Son of Encouragement (Acts 4:36). Leslie Flynn says, "Do we realize that, had not Barnabas used his gift of encouragement, we might be missing half the New Testament books?"[2]

Giving (or financial generosity) is the God-given ability to earn money and then give it liberally and cheerfully to God's work. I first saw this gift in action about five years after entering the ministry. One of the members of the church I pastored had been buying and selling surplus material as a hobby. Soon it became a major source of income and led him into a successful business with heavy equipment. About that time missionaries David and Alice Osborne visited the church, sharing their burden for an evangelistic center in a particular Japanese city. By the time the Osbornes reached their new location in Japan, two large tents were awaiting them. The surplus buyer had bought and shipped them at his expense to give them a tool for evangelism. The Kayashima Christian Center soon became a reality. On several other occasions I have introduced this generous man to family men who had been called to pastoral ministry. Bible college training seemed financially impossible. But each semester the college received a check to cover the tuition of one or more of these men. The gift of giving is too often left out of our list of important ministries.

Leadership (also translated authority or administration) is the ability to see God's direction for the church and to communicate this in such a way that the members work together to move in His direction. The gift of leadership enables a person to coordinate the gifts and ministries of others in the congregation for the good of all. For example, at a community church in Ogden, North Carolina the pastor believes every person has a ministry. Harold Crocker believes no one should be placed in an office simply because a vacancy exists. Using the gift of leadership, he helps members discover their own gifts and use them in appropriate positions in the church. Special care is given to assure that properly gifted people serve as deacons, since at Ogden the deacons are key people in evangelism.

The Greek word for leadership means helmsman, the person in charge of getting a ship to its destination. The owner decides where the ship is going, then hires a helmsman and provides him with a map or chart showing the route. The helmsman's responsibility is to make the necessary decisions and deal with obstacles along the way as he steers the ship so that it safely reaches the right port. The pastor may be like the owner of the ship. But it is not necessary for him to be the helmsman also. God may provide a capable layleader for this task.

Mercy (or kindness) is the God-given ability to show compassion for those who may be suffering from physical, mental, or emotional problems, and to do something to ease the suffering. The gift of encouraging relates to helping through words of love and kindness, while the gift of mercy refers to helping others through actions. While living in Detroit, I observed this gift in action. A six-year-old boy had contracted a debilitating disease that had damaged the nerves controlling muscle movements in his arms and legs. The doctors felt that the nerves could be reprogrammed if his arms and legs were moved in a particular pattern every four hours. The call for volunteers went out, and at first many people came to help. After several weeks, the task became tedious and most volunteers quit. But six Christians in the neighborhood stayed with the program. When I moved away eighteen months after the exercise program began, these six were still coming on schedule. I am convinced it took the gift of mercy to do this.

Why has God given such a rich variety of spiritual gifts to His church? Spiritual gifts are the church's tool kit for accomplishing ministry! Edification (building up one another) and evangelism are the twin purposes for the church. As each member uses his or her gifts, other members are built up. Members who have been edified become more effective witnesses to the pagan culture around them and can better evangelize their lost friends and neighbors. The uniqueness of the church's organization has been described this way: The church is not a *dictatorship* where one man rules; it is not a *democracy* where the will of the majority rules; it is not a *republic* where delegates rule. The church is an *organism* with Christ as the head and each member using his or her spiritual gifts for the benefit of the whole congregation. Does this describe your church? This study will help increase the effectiveness of your church in being what Christ expects His church to be.

Application

As you determine what your spiritual gifts may be, keep in mind the words of Peter in 1 Peter 4:10: "Each one should use whatever gift he has received to serve others, faithfully administering God's grace in its various forms." The practical reason for this is to keep us from becoming proud about our gifts or using them for selfish reasons. To keep your church functioning properly, your gifts must be used to serve others. Christ was the prime example of that lifestyle.

Remember the Christmas gift from my daughter? How excited I was as I opened that gift and realized that at last, by the sacrificial gift of somebody else, I had what was necessary to put my car in perfect running order. At last I could install that muffler. The sense of accomplishment in repairing the car was a thrill. An even greater thrill will come to Christian men and women who realize that they have been graciously equipped by Jesus Christ to provide the missing part for the lives of their neighbors.

3

Out of the stands: into the game

Christ has not called us to serve Him in our own
strength.

1 Corinthians 12:1-11

[1]Now about spiritual gifts, brothers, I do not want you to be ignorant. [2]You know that when you were pagans, somehow or other you were influenced and led astray to dumb idols. [3]Therefore I tell you that no one who is speaking by the Spirit of God says, "Jesus be cursed," and no one can say "Jesus is Lord," except by the Holy Spirit.

[4]There are different kinds of spiritual gifts, but the same Spirit. [5]There are different kinds of service, but the same Lord. [6]There are different kinds of working, but the same God works all of them in all men.

[7]Now to each one the manifestation of the Spirit is given for the common good. [8]To one there is given through the Spirit the message of wisdom, to another the message of knowledge by means of the same Spirit, [9]to another faith by the same Spirit, to another gifts of healing by that one Spirit, [10]to another miraculous powers, to another prophecy, to another the ability to distinguish between spirits, to another the ability to speak in different kinds of tongues, and to still another the interpretation of tongues. [11]All these are the work of one and the same Spirit, and He gives them to each one, just as He determines.

I think it was former Oklahoma football coach Bud Wilkinson who compared spectators in the stands with the players on the field. He said the few players out on the field desperately need rest whereas the thousands of spectators in the stands desperately need exercise. Does this describe your church? The biblical picture of the church is one of action on the part of all members. Dr. James Engel, head of the Department of Communication at Wheaton Graduate School, writes, "The biblical church has no benches on the sidelines of its playing field. The believer does not really have the option of moving to the sidelines in disobedience. John says, 'We know that we have come to know Him, if we obey His commands' (1 John 2:3)."[1]

In football, stamina, ability, and obedience keep a player in the game. For the Christian, natural talent and dynamic personality are not enough to fulfill the command to win lost men and women to Christ. Our limited abilities do not accomplish the task. Attempting to obey the command with only human resources leads to frustration, disappointment, and failure. But Christ has not called us to serve Him in our own strength. He has provided us with the tool kit of spiritual gifts. Properly understood and used, they make us capable servants who bring people to Christ and His church.

Several years ago a church in Haverhill, Massachusetts began to take on new life and growth after a long period of decline. Paul Bertolino, a mailman who had prepared for pastoral ministry, was called as pastor. The church's income was limited, so Pastor Paul kept his job with the post office. As membership increased, the Sunday School and youth ministries needed upgrading, but the pastor was not sure what should be done. So the church hired Gary Havener, a young man with gifts in this area, as assistant pastor.

Growth continued, and soon it became evident that more time must be given to administering church affairs. Pastor Paul would have to give up some of the time spent using his gifts of preaching and counseling. But wait—Bob Wilson, a Christian who worked for the local fire department, had demonstrated gifts of administration in a nearby church. At the time his gifts were not being used there. Would he take on the responsibility of helping the church set goals in keeping with God's purpose and lead them in accomplishing them? He would, and he did.

At least two more persons were added to the staff as new areas of need and service became apparent. Through all this, the senior pastor still was part time. One of the young men was paid full time, and others were hired part time. That is nonconformity. But it proved to be an effective way for Christians to be God's servants in Haverhill. The result? The church grew tremendously. The auditorium and overflow space is full Sundays. The expanding Sunday School holds classes in the nearby mental health center as well as in every available space in the church building. Recently, the church helped parent a new congregation a few miles away in Plaistow, New Hampshire. This temporarily reduced attendance, since thirty members formed the new congregation. The church continues to touch new families, and now is planning a new branch in Bradford. Bob Wilson and Pastor Paul testify that members willing to use their spiritual gifts are a key to growth for them. That is nonconformity.

Helping church members discover and use their spiritual gifts will not automatically bring growth; nevertheless, unless a church recognizes and uses the ministry of every member, growth will be impossible. The Apostle Paul was a firm believer in the every-member ministry. In chapter 2 we saw seven spiritual gifts mentioned in Paul's letter to the church at Rome. Perhaps you discovered you have one of those gifts. There are two other lists in Paul's writings, and you're likely to find another gift or two of yours there.

Bible Base

Read 1 Corinthians 12:1-11. The church at Corinth was young, growing rapidly, and situated in a very immoral city. Paul had founded the church on his second missionary tour. The church members were basically non-Jewish converts from paganism. They did not have the advantage of the rich heritage of the Old Testament as did Jewish converts. To keep them in proper perspective regarding spiritual gifts, Paul covers the subject in detail in 1 Corinthians chapters 12—14.

"I do not want you to be ignorant." In their case, ignorance about spiritual gifts was causing the Corinthians to be over-zealous concerning some gifts. This lack of understanding about the gifts keeps some churches from making disciples. It can cause Christians to feel discouraged, insecure, frustrated, and guilty because they feel they are not effective for God.

Bill had sung in a Gospel group for several years, until a diseased lung had to be removed. One day he began crying in my office. His heart was broken because his singing career was ended and he could no longer be of use to the Lord. After praying with him, I began discussing spiritual gifts. He acknowledged that after every concert during his ten years with the group, people would come to him with burdens and problems. After he counseled them from Scripture and prayed with them, the people seemed to be helped and went away rejoicing. I was able to confirm the gift of encouragement in Bill's life, and he was radiant. The illness had placed him on disability pay, and he spent several hours each day seeking out people in the community who needed encouragement. Knowing and using your gift can bring you the same sense of joy and fulfillment.

The Corinthians could readily identify with the situation in 1 Corinthians 12:3. The pagans in Corinth cried out, "Jesus be cursed!" whenever they saw a known Christian, or when they tried to break up a service. The Christians responded, "Jesus is Lord!" The apostle says it is only those possessed by the Holy Spirit who can say from the heart, "Jesus is Lord!" Christians are not identified by names or creeds or churches, but rather by the presence of the Holy Spirit in their lives. Jesus emphasized the importance of this relationship: "I will ask the Father, and He will give you another Counselor to be with you forever—the Spirit of truth. The world cannot accept Him, because it neither sees Him nor knows Him. But you know Him, for He lives with you and will be in you" (John 14:16-17).

I saw a demonstration of what saying "Jesus is Lord!" means at Arizona State University. A friend and I were walking across the campus to see the Grady Gammage Auditorium. A Hare Krishna group was out in force in gauze robes and shaved heads. Near the auditorium entrance one of them engaged us in a discussion. After about ten minutes, my friend John said, "You don't have the Spirit of the true God in you; you can't say 'Jesus is Lord.'"

The young man immediately said, "Jesus is Lord!" What were we to do? Was the Scripture wrong?

Beckoning to some other Hare Krishna people, John pointed to the student talking with us and shouted, "One of your converts just said 'Jesus is Lord!'" That student ran from us with the speed of a 100-yard-dash track sprinter. He was not saying, "Jesus is Lord" from the heart.

The Corinthians needed to know that all the gifts and workings of those gifts have the same source, and in chapter 12, verses 4-6 he points out that it is the same Spirit, the same Lord, and the same God expressing all the gifts in and through us. Spiritual gifts are for the common good, not for personal use or enrichment. They are gifts to the church.

Some of the spiritual gifts may seem to be more important than others, but Paul stresses that as they work together they are of equal importance. They have the same Source, God; they have the same purpose, the good of the whole church; and they are determined and distributed by the same Source, the Holy Spirit. There is no need for us to beg and plead for a particular gift. It is our responsibility to discover what gifts God has already given us through the Holy Spirit, and then to get busy learning how to use those gifts for the ministry of our church.

In Romans 12 we discovered these spiritual gifts: prophecy, service, teaching, encouraging, giving, leadership, and mercy. First Corinthians 12:8-10 mentions one of these again and adds eight more. Turn back to the passage at the beginning of this chapter on page 34 and circle the new gifts.

Implication

Each time the New Testament talks about gifts, the ones mentioned are related to a particular need or problem. No two lists contain the same gifts. This is because the gifts named are suggestive, not exhaustive. Several other gifts are mentioned in various New Testament books: celibacy, hospitality, voluntary poverty, just to mention a few. Then there is the gift you only use once, given in 1 Corinthians 13:3— martyrdom! Many people would list prayer as a gift too. While all Christians pray, there are some who seem to have unusual ability to concentrate in prayer for long periods of time, and see their prayers answered in amazing ways.

Amaranathy, a young Christian woman in India, has this gift. As a child she was a boarding student in the Advent Christian school in Guindy. After completing high school, she turned away from the Lord. A few years later she rededicated her life to Christ, and the Holy Spirit gave her the gift of prayer. She used this gift to minister in her neighborhood. She prayed for friends who had tried unsuccessfully for months to find work, and soon jobs opened. Several women in the church had not been able to have children. Following prayer by Aramanathy, they soon became pregnant. Wherever she went, God used her ministry of prayer. Today she assists her pastor-husband, who is establishing a new church near Madras.

As you read the definitions of the following gifts, compare them carefully with 1 Corinthians 12:8-10. Determine which of these gifts the Holy Spirit may have given you. Remember that verse 11 says we have all received at least one gift, if we know Christ as Saviour and Lord.

Wisdom is the ability given to some Christians to apply spiritual truth to complex situations with good results, and to apply knowledge to specific needs in the church. Have you ever sat through a church business meeting for hours as two different opinions were discussed and no progress toward a decision was forthcoming? Then a brother or sister rises and makes a new suggestion about the matter, and immediately the whole group senses it to be the right course to follow. That person has used the gift of wisdom.

Knowledge is the special ability from God to discover, analyze, understand, and make clear to others ideas and information that will improve the life and ministry of the church. Persons with the gift of knowledge are avid learners. They enjoy studying and reasoning through difficult problems. Usually they have great patience with their work. The gift of knowledge is tremendously helpful for those involved in Bible translation. Often human knowledge is at a loss for a word in some native dialect that will adequately express the meaning of a New Testament Greek word. But through direct impression on the mind or by circumstances God makes the translator aware of how to phrase it. *In Other Words,* a publication of Wycliffe Bible Translators, provides many examples of the gift of knowledge at work in this way.

Faith is the gift that enables some Christians to see clearly what God wants to accomplish and to work at that goal in spite of any obstacles. This isn't saving faith; all Christians have that. This kind of faith is taking God at His word and doing something about it. *The Living Bible* paraphrase of Hebrews 11:1 is graphic: "What is faith? It is the confident assurance that something we want is going to happen. It is the certainty that what we hope for is waiting for us, even though we cannot see it up ahead."

George Muller, founder of orphanages in England, had this gift. With no apparent source of money for food, he regularly received additional unwanted children into the homes. At times the evening mealtime would come, and no food was available. Muller would gather the children to the table and offer the blessing. His prayer would be interrupted by a knock at the door. The caller would deliver milk and bread, vegetables, or some other food in quantity sufficient to feed the children.

Missionary Julia Lake Kellersberger has this gift. My family has been at her home when fifteen or twenty guests would show up within a few minutes of mealtime. Undaunted, she would invite them for a meal, even though she only had enough food for four or five. Hardly was the invitation accepted by the guests when a fisherman on the river called to see if she could use a large catch of fish; a neighbor called to offer several bushel of grapefruit and oranges that were too ripe to ship to market; the bread truck stopped at just that moment, and the driver asked if she could use six loaves of day-old bread. In thirty minutes Julia Lake's guests had a suitable banquet. This was a lifestyle with her. She believed the more she gave away, the more her Heavenly Father would provide.

Healing is the ability to bring spiritual, emotional, or physical healing to a person apart from the use of natural means. This gift does not give a person special power over sickness; he or she simply becomes a channel God uses when He desires to heal. Often James 5:14-15 forms the pattern for its use.

Miracles is the gift of being used by God to perform acts that cannot be explained by natural laws and that require power beyond one's own. Our Western culture has taught us to be suspicious of anything we can't explain or perform through our own knowledge and strength. Do not close your mind to God's daily miracles.

Distinguishing between spirits is the God-given ability to know whether a particular teaching or behavior is of God or Satan. Those with this gift are needed today, with the multitude of cults that are flooding our land. Apparently many of the people who followed Jim Jones to Guiana and ended their lives at his urging came out of Christian backgrounds. The gift of distinguishing between spirits enabled many to realize that this man had become a tool of Satan. Paul shows the need for this gift in 2 Corinthians 11:13-15.

Tongues is the gift of being able to speak in a language that you have not learned. This is the most controversial of the gifts. In 1 Corinthians 14, Paul suggests two kinds, or uses, of the gift: to speak to God in a language you have never learned, and to communicate a message from God to the congregation in a language you have not learned.

Interpretation of tongues is the ability God gives to interpret a language you do not understand for the benefit of the church. Paul's first letter to the church at Corinth was written to deal with problems of excess in this young congregation. In chapter 14, verses 27 and 28, he points out that a message in an unknown tongue does not build up the congregation unless there is interpretation in the known tongue.

Some churches believe the gifts of tongues and interpretation are for every age, while others think that they were for the first century only. What does your church teach?

Application

"You have everything when you have Christ" (Colossians 2:10, TLB). In West Texas there is a famous oil field known as Yates Pool. During the Depression, Mr. Yates had a sheep ranch there. All through those hard years, Yates worried about how he would be able to pay his bills. What if he had to sell his ranch?

Then an oil company exploration team came to West

Texas. They asked permission to drill a test well on his ranch. He signed a lease contract, and drilling began. At 1,115 feet, they struck oil. The first well produced 80,000 barrels a day, and additional ones had an even greater flow. Yates owned it all. When he purchased the land, he also got the oil and mineral rights. During those years of near-starvation, he had been grazing sheep on acres of black gold because he didn't know the oil was there.

You and I are like that at times. We miss some of the rich satisfaction in life and in our church work because we have not discovered the spiritual tool kit God has provided for us— our spiritual gifts.

4

Frozen assets
under the steeple

All members of the church are clergy. God's people
includes all members of the church, not merely a
special group called clergy.

Ephesians 4:11-16; 5:1-2

It was He who gave some to be apostles, some to be prophets, some to be evangelists, and some to be pastors and teachers, [12]to prepare God's people for works of service, so that the body of Christ may be built up [13]until we all reach unity in the faith and in the knowledge of the Son of God and become mature, attaining to the whole measure of the fullness of Christ.

[14]Then we will no longer be infants, tossed back and forth by the waves, and blown here and there by every wind of teaching and by the cunning and craftiness of men in their deceitful scheming. [15]Instead, speaking the truth in love, we will in all things grow up into Him who is the Head, that is, Christ. [16]From Him the whole body, joined and held together by every supporting ligament, grows and builds itself up in love, as each part does its work.

Be imitators of God, therefore, as dearly loved children and live a life of love, just as Christ loved us and gave Himself up for us as a fragrant offering and sacrifice to God.

According to Elton Trueblood, "The church is intended as a concrete answer to the prayer that laborers be sent forth to the harvest. The company of Jesus is not people streaming to a shrine; and it is not people making up an audience for a speaker; it is laborers engaged in the harvesting task of reaching their perplexed and seeking brethren with something so vital that, if received, it will change their lives."[1]

During the past few years I have visited churches where members have been involved in harvesting. Since 1981 most churches in our fellowship have participated in "Harvest Now! Our Thrust in Evangelism." We have awakened to the fact that we are the answer to the prayer Christ commanded us to pray, that the Lord of the harvest would send out workers into His harvest field. Torrington, Connecticut; Dover, Florida; State Road, Maine; Lewiston, Idaho; and LaGrange, Illinois are representative of congregations who are putting the *Go* into the Gospel. Members are being instructed in how to bear witness, how to counsel persons with needs, how to disciple new converts and bring them into the fellowship of the church, and how to discover just who makes up the mission field.

The "many-members, one-body, everybody-working-

49

concept" should have been operative in the church since the days of Luther. There were two key emphases in the Protestant Reformation: salvation by faith alone, and the priesthood of all believers. Somehow Luther and his comrades took one step and made salvation by faith alone the foundation for Protestantism. But they never took the other step, practicing the priesthood of believers. I suppose we shouldn't criticize Luther too harshly for that. The Roman Church had taught for years that the clergy had all the intelligence, and the laity went about like animals with no minds of their own. Luther faced the task of moving ahead with an organization quickly, and there was not time to train totally uneducated laymen for participation in the life of the church. The doctrine of the priesthood of believers was forgotten in the shuffle.

The last fourth of the twentieth century may well be called the Protestant Reformation, Part Two. Significant steps are being taken to make the priesthood of all believers a reality. Members of the congregation are being trained and used for a variety of functions formerly reserved for the clergy. One California church has laypeople handling most hospital visitation. At Prophetstown, Illinois, the laity is visiting in homes of families moving into the community.

How did most of the members of the church become "frozen assets"? The word clergy comes from the Greek *kleros,* and laity is the English translation of *laos. Kleros* refers to calling. It is used in 1 Corinthians 1:2, "To the church of God in Corinth . . . *called* to be holy." All members of the church are clergy, God's called people. When used in relation to God's new community in Christ, it means the group of people who are redeemed through Christ, not a special group of leaders called clergy. *Laos* means people, referring to the chosen people of God. It is used twice in 1 Peter 2:10: "Once you were not a *people,* but now you are the *people* of God." (Italics added.)

What would happen in your church if every member discovered he or she was both laity and clergy? If you have 175 members, you'd instantly grow from having 1 minister to having 176. You could then perform more effectively the work of the Great Commission. What are we waiting for? Let's take action and join the Every-Member-a-Minister movement today!

Bible Base

Read Ephesians 4:11-16. Verse 11 lists some gifts that are important for support, order, and growth in the church: apostles, prophets, evangelists, and pastor-teachers. They are given in title form rather than function form. The prophet is the title for a person who functions with the gift of prophecy. Paul has already taught us that all gifts are important. These four relate more to the total membership than some of the others, and help provide the framework within which the church experiences healthy increase. For this reason these gifts are more likely to be seen in the ordained leaders: pastors; missionaries; conference, regional, and national church officers.

Did the gift of *apostle* end with the original Twelve plus Matthias? (Acts 1:15-26) Some Bible scholars think so. But later in the Book of Acts and in Paul's letters the term is used in a much broader way. Paul is not mentioned in the original list, yet he became an apostle (Rom. 1:1; 1 Cor. 9:1; 2 Cor. 12:12). Barnabas too served as an apostle (Acts 14:14). Others mentioned as apostles include Andronicus and Junias (Rom. 16:7), James the Lord's brother (Gal. 1:19), and Silvanus and Timothy (1 Thes. 1:1; 2:7). After the New Testament era, the office of apostle was still recognized in the church.

The gift of apostle is the God-given ability to declare the foundational truth about Jesus Christ in such a way that people recognize it as clear teaching about God. People with this gift make capable leaders over several congregations. They also may be effective in planting new churches. Apostleship is vital for your church's evangelism ministry. Adoniram Judson was an apostle to Burma, William Carey to India, Hudson Taylor to China, and Frank Toothe to China, Japan, and the Philippines.

In chapter 2 we elaborated on the gift of *prophecy*. Prophecy comes from a Greek word meaning to cause to shine. Ray Stedman explains the difference between apostle and prophet this way:

"The apostle gives an authoritative declaration of the whole body of truth concerning Jesus Christ; but the prophet interprets that authoritative word and explains the truth so that it becomes very clear, vital, and compelling."[2]

Ephesians 4:11 also mentions the gift of *evangelism*. Here is the primary gift for church growth. It is the God-given ability to share the Gospel with people in such a way that they receive Christ as Saviour and become members of His church. It is *not* more important than the other gifts. Evangelism fulfills the Great Commission only when the other gifts are operating in the church.

Each year I take some vacation time to participate in a canoe trip through the Okefenokee Swamp and down the Suwannee River in southeast Georgia and Florida. The 165 miles of paddling requires strong arms. They hold up for the entire trip only because my mouth regularly chews food, my stomach digests it, my body assimilates it, and my arm muscles derive their strength from this process. Similarly, the gift of evangelism is effective in your church when the gifts of prophecy, service, teaching, leadership, mercy, and the others we have studied are working harmoniously.

Sometimes the gift of evangelism is used as a Christian's vocation. Leighton Ford, one of today's great evangelists, travels all over the world evangelizing, and the church is blessed as disciples are made. For others, the gift is used as the Lord provides opportunities at work and in the neighborhood.

My friend Jack Mumpower in Atlanta works for the telephone company. He has the gift of evangelism. At lunch hour, coffee breaks, and similar times the Lord brings fellow employees to his table or desk, and they often ask for advice or counsel with a problem. The Spirit guides Jack to naturally deal with spiritual matters in the course of the conversation, and often the result is a decision for Christ or an invitation to Jack's house to talk further about the Lord. Whenever I pass through Atlanta, I call Jack to learn of recent conversions as he uses his gift, and my heart thrills as he reports. More of us with the gift of evangelism are needed who will minister as Jack does.

Churches that show a steady increase in conversions have approximately 8-10 percent of the membership using the gift of evangelism on the job, in the neighborhood, and in the church. Where the pastor is the only one doing the work of evangelism, there may be little or no membership increase. How many people in your congregation have the gift of evangelism?

Be careful not to confuse the *role* of witness itself with the *gift* of evangelism. Every Christian has a personal relationship with Jesus Christ, and that relationship needs to be shared whenever we have opportunity. Our faithful witness to what Christ has done for us in saving us and is now doing in guiding and strengthening us lays a foundation for the evangelist to use in leading people to Christ and becoming a part of His church. The fact that we may not sense that we have the *gift* of evangelism is not a valid excuse for not regularly witnessing about what the living Lord means to us.

The final gift in verse 11 is that of *pastor-teacher*. This is a combination gift. Pastoring refers to the ability to feed, guide, and minister to a group of believers. There are three New Testament terms which describe this gift: *shepherd* describes what one does, *overseer* refers to how one does it, and *elder* refers to the pastor's place in the church. They involve the building up and growth of the church. Teaching refers to the main method the pastor uses under God to build up the church.

Verse 12 gives the job description for persons with these gifts, especially the pastor-teacher, since he or she likely has a long-term relationship with the members of the church. The following diagram will clarify verse 12:

Apostles	have	to prepare
Prophets	this	God's people
Evangelists	task	
Pastor-teachers		

| for | works of service | so that | the body of Christ may be built up |

Notice how these four gifts work together. The apostle declares the truth about Jesus Christ, the prophet explains and makes it clear, the evangelist guides people in responding to Christ, and the pastor-teacher helps them grow as Christians and learn how to share their newfound faith with others. What a practical cycle!

During 1977 I visited India. On a hot afternoon a group of us went to the seashore not far from Madras. I tired from bucking the waves and sat near a fishing boat while waiting for the rest of the group. Two fishermen came to the boat and pulled out a large net and spread it on the ground. Carefully, they checked each section and retied several strands. If they were to make a good catch of fish the next day, they had to mend the tears in the net caused by that day's heavy use.

Paul had this picture in mind when he wrote to the Christians at Ephesus. They would be familiar with the task of mending the nets. Similarly, the pastor-teacher is called and gifted to mend the saints and get them ready for action. Part of that mending includes helping them discover, develop, and use their spiritual gifts.

Verses 12-16 provide a profile of the person who has been properly prepared and developed in the church:

1. *Productive.* Verse 12, prepared "for works of service, so that the body of Christ may be built up."

2. *In harmony.* Verse 13, sensing a oneness with the other members through a common understanding of the faith.

3. *Mature.* Verse 13b, an evident Christlikeness indicating spiritual growth.

4. *Stable.* Verse 14, moving away from childish tangents.

5. *Truthful*. Verse 15, living the truth we claim to believe.

6. *Working together*. Verse 16, realizing that God is glorified as we use our gifts in cooperation with the other members.

The twin tasks of the church are: building up Christians and evangelizing pagans. Perry and Lias describe a congregation with a healthy balance, "A people devoted to prayer, intercession, thanksgiving, and praise; a testifying, witnessing membership which speaks in the boldness of the Spirit in the church, home, school, and shop. The membership should be devoted to a sacrifice of time, treasure, and talents. Labor to achieve a membership which is Spirit-filled. Likewise, Bible-centered and Bible-studying, given to daily Bible study and devotion. The pastor and the entire membership should become progressively missionary-minded, heeding the admonition, 'Go ye into all the world and preach the Gospel.' "³

Ephesians 5:1-2 belongs to the discussion of chapter 4. The word *therefore* reminds us of this. Christians using spiritual gifts in a productive, harmonious, mature way are imitating Christ in His world!

One summer I taught John 15 to senior high students at Blowing Rock Camp in North Carolina. One day, bursts of laughter came every few minutes from the 25 teens, although I saw nothing to laugh about. Curiosity finally got the best of me, and I whirled around to see if someone was behind me. Sure enough, there was the cook's nine-year-old son in the doorway. He had been doing a magnificent job of mimicking my gestures. Paul tells us to observe the spirit in which Christ lived and ministered and, using our gifts, mimic that spirit as we live daily. Then we will be pleasing and satisfactory to God. Spiritual gifts have been called the church's *frozen assets*. It is time to thaw them out and use them.

Application

Is your pastor the only person in your church using spiritual gifts? How can you discover and develop yours without some models? Many Christians are already using gifts to a limited degree, even if they have not called them by name. Are you a teacher, deacon, trustee, member of the hospitality committee, or leader of some group in the church? You may have been selected because other members saw that you were gifted for that service.

Keep these two things in mind as you search for God's gifts to you. First, spiritual gifts are given only to Christians. Everyone is born with natural talents and abilities and uses these in earning a living and influencing others in similar, natural ways. But only Christians are given special abilities by the Holy Spirit to enable them to produce growth and unity in their church. Peter's counsel to the church was: "Each one should use whatever gift he has received to serve others, faithfully administering God's grace in its various forms" (1 Peter 4:10). Do you know Christ personally? Do you have assurance of your salvation? If so, you are ready to continue. If not, this would be an appropriate time to receive Him as Saviour. Then you can confidently search for the gifts He has for you.

Second, pray regularly for God to give you insight as you seek to discover and use your gifts. James 1:5 says, "If any of you lacks wisdom, he should ask God, who gives generously to all." God is more willing to give gifts to us than we are to ask for them. He is glorified and we are strengthened for service when we learn what our gifts are and begin to use them. Are you ready to discover which ones the Holy Spirit has distributed to you? Take a moment to pray for His guidance in this exciting quest.

Dr. C. Peter Wagner, of Fuller Theological Seminary, suggests five steps for discovering your gifts. These will guide you in your search:

Step One: Explore the possibilities.
Chapters 2-4 of this book have led you in Bible study relating to gifts. Read all the Scriptures you can find on the subject. Comparing the passages in several translations would be helpful: *King James, New American Standard, New International Version,* and *Today's English Version.* Discuss the

subject with your pastor to discover his gifts and the church's position on gifts. Discuss the matter with others in your church. And read some good books.

Step Two: Experiment with as many as you can.
Bill Nash was anxious to get active in the life of his church. He began experimenting with gifts. When his Sunday School class teacher went on vacation for two weeks, he offered to be the substitute. The first Sunday half the class fell asleep and the second week most stayed home. Teaching was not his gift. Mrs. Dewlap was ill and in the hospital, so he stopped by to visit with her. As he prayed for her healing, she had another stroke and died. Healing wasn't his gift either.

Pastor Jones took Bill with him to visit a new family in the community. Bill soon began regular meetings with the couple, and in less than a month they prayed to receive Christ as Saviour. The pastor began referring other prospects to him, and several became Christians through his ministry. Bill found his gift: evangelism.

You can start by looking for some things that need doing around your church. Volunteer to do some of them. Accept any tasks assigned to you. Ask the Lord to show you through that experience if it represents your gift. Make a note of the gifts you discover you do not have. That narrows the field. Have you been a substitute teacher and 90 percent of the class fell asleep? Probably teaching is not one of your gifts. Try visiting sick and shut-ins, chairing committees, providing lodging for visiting missionaries, and any other ideas the Lord brings to mind.

Step Three: Examine your feelings.
Don't fall for the trap that if you are enjoying something, it must not be God's will for you. That is a common idea among Christians, but it is not biblical. If you enjoy something, your performance of that task is better than if you dread it. That's why God reserves the right to decide what our spiritual gifts will be, rather than allowing us to choose. He knows what we

are best fitted for, and His way brings the greatest joy and blessing. When you feel excited and happy about a particular work you are doing for God, you probably have discovered one of your spiritual gifts.

Step Four: Evaluate your effectiveness.
God gives gifts to help us carry out His work in the church and in the world. As you discover increased effectiveness in using a particular gift, that will be an indication you have found one of your gifts. Ask these questions about the particular ministry or service you are performing:

1. Am I becoming more competent in the use of this gift?
2. Do I have regular opportunities to use this gift?
3. Are others being helped by my service?

If you have the gift of evangelism, people will come to Christ as a result of your witness to them. If your gift is administration, the organization runs well. If your gift is healing, people get well when you pray. Because your gift is from God and has His strength behind it, you will be effective when you use the gift.

Step Five: Expect confirmation.
Spiritual gifts are given for use within the church, so other members will be aware when you are using your gift. This is the most important step. Amna Shelley, a deaconess in Blessed Hope Church in Detroit, has the gift of mercy. She is a retired nurse and has combined that ability with her gift. Members of the church sense her gift, and regularly refer to her persons in the community who need special attention: the ill, shut-ins, retarded, and unwed mothers. And Amna's use of her gift blesses those she serves.

Let's evaluate ourselves in view of the gifts we've studied. Read the definitions given in chapters 2, 3, and 4 for each gift listed below. In the second column indicate any situations you can think of where you have used this gift. You'll leave some blanks. In the right-hand column list any opportunities you can think of where the gifts could be used within your church and its programs.

Gift	How I have used it	Opportunities for use in my church
Prophecy		
Service		
Teaching		
Encouraging		
Giving		
Leadership		
Mercy		
Wisdom		
Knowledge		
Faith		
Healing		
Miracles		
Distinguishing spirits		
Tongues		
Interpretation of tongues		
Apostleship		
Evangelism		
Pastor-teacher		

5

A crash course in fishing

You must decide what kind of fish you want to catch.

1 Corinthians 9:19-22

¹⁹Though I am free and belong to no man, I make myself a slave to everyone, to win as many as possible. ²⁰To the Jews I became like a Jew, to win the Jews. To those under the Law I became like one under the Law . . . so as to win those under the Law. ²¹To those not having the Law I became like one not having the Law. ²²To the weak I became weak, to win the weak. I have become all things to all men so that by all possible means I might save some.

1 Corinthians 10:31-33

³¹So whether you eat or drink or whatever you do, do it all for the glory of God. ³²Do not cause anyone to stumble, whether Jews, Greeks, or the church of God—³³even as I try to please everybody in every way. For I am not seeking my own good but the good of many, so that they may be saved.

1 Corinthians 4:1-2

¹So then, men ought to regard us as servants of Christ and as those entrusted with the secret things of God. ²Now it is required that those who have been given a trust must prove faithful.

Matthew 25:19-21, 24-26

¹⁹"After a long time the master of those servants returned and settled accounts with them. ²⁰The man who had received the five talents brought the other five. 'Master,' he said, 'you entrusted me with five talents. See, I have gained five more.'

²¹His master replied, 'Well done, good and faithful servant! You have been faithful with a few things; I will put you in charge of many things. Come and share your master's happiness!'

²⁴"Then the man who had received the one talent came. 'Master,' he said, ' . . . I was afraid and went out and hid your talent . . . .'

²⁶"His master replied, 'You wicked, lazy servant!' "

Everyone expected the 1980 Republican Convention to be boring. After all, Ronald Reagan was assured of votes from an overwhelming majority of the delegates. The major TV channels were broadcasting it, yet many people preferred the excitement of their usual programs. That was true at least until 10:15 P.M. on Wednesday, July 16. At that moment Paul Laxalt let the cat out of the bag; Ronald Reagan had been in conference much of the evening with former President Gerald Ford concerning his becoming the vice-presidential candidate. The Reagan people felt a Reagan-Ford ticket would be hard to beat.

But Mr. Ford was willing to run only if the vice president became, in reality, a co-president with special authority over the National Security Council, and if Reagan would find a spot for Henry Kissinger in the Cabinet. That was too great a price to pay. Candidate Reagan switched to Plan B, and George Bush became his running mate. The rest is history.

Your church may not reach its goal if you have only one plan. Sometimes Plan A is not realistic, and even extreme effort will not bring success. Let's assume a church in a nearby city sets the goal of winning all the lost in the community to Christ. This is a hazy goal—how can you measure it? A goal of identifying and reaching for Christ fifty lost people in a five-block area around the church would be a better goal. The Scripture does not promise that everyone will receive Christ.

Political candidates don't usually put all their efforts into one method. They use media advertising, block and precinct leaders, rallies, and a host of other tools. This is a good example for us in the church to follow. Instead of just relying on an annual August revival campaign, let's have weekly visitation during the fall and winter and a Sunday School enlargement campaign in the spring. Does your church have more than just Plan A?

Bible Base

How can we reach our world? The Apostle Paul has some words for us.

Read 1 Corinthians 9:12-22. Paul is expressing the depth of concern he felt for the lost. This is not just another way of saying, "When in Rome do as the Romans do." He suggests that we look for ways to approach people where they are without being obnoxious about it. For instance, Paul's witness to Greeks would not have gotten far if his first statement to them was that circumcision was necessary before they could find salvation. Yet Paul circumcised Timothy because he knew Jews would be turned off if his traveling companion, a Jew (with a Gentile father), was not circumcised. If Paul were alive today and was going to New York or Los Angeles to minister, he would learn the customs of the people and live by them as long as it did not compromise his faith.

Paul establishes a principle for us all: "Whatever you do, do it all for the glory of God" (1 Cor. 10:31). Think of the things you will be doing this week. Whether you will be working with people or things, how can you do them all in a way that will bring glory to God? Two aspects of glorifying God are given in connection with this principle: "Do not cause anyone to stumble," and "so that they may be saved."

First Corinthians 4:1-2 deals with responsibility and accountability. The Greek word for servants means under-rower.

Paul pictures a large ship with rowers on three levels. The under-rowers were way down in the galley. They could not see where the ship was going; they just obeyed the commands of their superior. We are under orders from a higher authority, Jesus Christ. Being "entrusted with the secret things of God" refers to the character of our service. You and I are trustees of the Gospel—it is Christ's Gospel, not ours. Our responsibility is to use it as our Master intended, recognizing that He is our superior officer and we are the under-rowers.

The passage in Matthew 25 from the Parable of the Talents illustrates what Christ expects from faithful stewards or trustees of His Gospel. The Parable of the Ten Virgins comes just before this, stressing the need for careful preparation for Christ's second coming. The audience who heard this parable could understand the illustration from the world of commerce. An accounting is expected from trustees. The servants who received five talents and two talents and doubled their master's money were rewarded with praise for doing the proper thing. The servant who received one talent and hid it was scolded: "You wicked, lazy servant!" The master then said that the servant should have at least put the talent in the bank to draw interest if he wasn't able to think of a more creative way to increase its value.

Do you see the application? The Parable of the Talents illustrates what 1 Corinthians 4:2 means: "It is required that those who have been given a trust must prove faithful." The earthly master entrusted his steward with his resources, to use them faithfully to bring a good return. Jesus Christ has entrusted His Gospel to us and expects us to use it faithfully to bring a good return on its purpose. Faithful servants are successful stewards, and a key determinant of our success or failure is the return to the goal of the Gospel. Romans 1:16 says the goal of the Gospel is the salvation of everyone who believes.

Implication

Think about some *methods* good stewards might use in

making disciples. Percy Deverick of Lenoir, North Carolina may not know it, but he has taught me something about methods of New Testament evangelism. I attended a course he offered in fly tying and techniques of fishing in mountain streams. He laid down some basic principles at the beginning:

1. You must decide what kind of fish you want to catch. It takes different bait and a different kind of rod to catch trout than it does smallmouth bass.

2. You must learn where and when to catch each variety. Many fish won't bite during the heat of the day. Some are more easily caught in the early morning, others just before dark.

3. You must know the right size hook and strength of line for each fish.

4. You must know which fish are caught around rocks and weeds, near the surface, on the bottom; which are best caught by casting or trolling, and how to move the bait or lure through the water.

In the classes, I got insights on how to be more successful at winning people for Jesus Christ. People are no more alike than are fish. To evangelize my community, I need to know what the people are like, what interests they have, what their social and cultural backgrounds are, what they believe, and how much they already know about the Gospel.

What methods is your church using to evangelize your community? Make a list of them. Then jot down after each one the names of the people who have come to Christ in the past five years as a result of using each method. Good stewards of the Gospel will regularly evaluate their methods. If any method is not working to the glory of God and the extension of the kingdom, drop it and find a method that will accomplish that purpose. In view of Christ's near return, we do not have time to work with outdated tools just because we have been using them for the past forty years. "It is required that those who have been given a trust must prove faithful" (1 Cor. 4:2).

A church in Pasadena, California is experimenting with new

methods. For many years they did traditional ministry. This was fine as the make-up of the church did not change from generation to generation. But a few years ago part of their community was settled by black families, and more recently Hispanics have also moved into the area. Efforts to reach the blacks had brought no results. How could anything be done with the Hispanics, many of whom spoke only Spanish?

Someone remembered that Ed Pitts, who had grown up in the Los Angeles church, was a vice-president of Laubach Literacy International. A letter to that organization brought word of their English for Speakers of Other Languages program. The Pasadena church contacted an area representative. After several meetings, the church learned that many Hispanics were unemployed because they could not read and write English. This kept them from applying for jobs. Church members with gifts of teaching and helps were trained in the Laubach method and tutored the Hispanics. About the same time, Carlos Quintero, a Panamanian student at Fuller Seminary, offered to conduct Spanish-language worship services. Because the church showed interest in helping with the learning of English, Hispanic families began attending worship, and a healthy, growing Hispanic congregation now meets in the chapel.

Another church member with the gift of evangelism started calling on black families. Soon a home was opened for weekly Bible study and fifteen-twenty-five people meet regularly to learn about the Bible and Christ. Several teens and adults have been won to Christ through the home meetings and are now active in the church. The home Bible study for blacks and Spanish-language service for Hispanics continue to be effective tools for reaching new neighbors for Christ. The church is finding the process of assimilating black and Hispanic converts into the mainstream of church life one that needs special care and sensitivity. Members with gifts of leadership, wisdom, and helps are particularly important at this point.

When fishing for lost people, keep these principles in mind:

1. Decide whom you are trying to reach.
2. Determine their interests and needs.
3. Develop plans.
4. Do it.
5. Decisions will be the result.

At some point we all learn that methods don't work; people work, using methods. You may have attended a Lay Institute for Evangelism and learned all about the witnessing method using "The Four Spiritual Laws" made popular by Campus Crusade for Christ. I carry one of the "Four Laws" booklets with me all the time, but as long as it is in my shirt pocket it does not help me to lead people to Christ. Once in a while as I conduct a community strategy study for a church, I'll meet an individual who seems especially open to my discussion of the church and her work. Then I pull out the booklet and use it as a tool to explain the plan of salvation. And in about one time out of three, the person will pray to receive Christ. The method didn't work—I worked, using a spiritual gift and a method.

What is our *motivation* for reaching our world? The loftiest reason we could think of would be that we share Christ out of gratitude for what He has done for us. The grace of God was one of Paul's key themes: "I am the least of the apostles and do not even deserve to be called an apostle. . . . But by the grace of God I am what I am" (1 Cor. 15:9-10). First Corinthians 4 points out that we've been entrusted with the Gospel and Christ expects us to be faithful in sharing it.

Somehow the affluence around us and the welfare programs to care for those who aren't affluent have caused us to lose some of the burden for the lost that was felt by our forefathers when they read 1 John 5:12: "He who has the Son has life; he who does not have the Son of God does not have life." Some of my neighbors are not Christians. But they are moral people, they don't get in trouble, and would be considered "very good" by the world's standards. It is too easy for me to allow this to cool my passion to see them come to know Christ as I know Him. Have you ever experienced this problem?

When I realize the inner peace and strength I derive from a daily relationship with Christ and the joy I have found since making Him the center of my life, I am moved to share Him with friends in the hope that they too can experience this. Outwardly, it seems that prosperity has closed people's minds to considering the claims of Christ. In reality many people around you face each day with a quiet desperation within. According to John R. Mott, "Times such as these plow up men's souls and make them ready for the planting of the seed of the Gospel."

At times the Christian's response to witnessing is, "Let George do it." This phrase originated with pilots in World War II when they switched their planes to automatic pilot, which they called "George." It has become our way of saying we want someone else to do our work. However, George does not have spiritual gifts; people do. So we should thank God for the gifts He has given us to make us useful members of the evangelistic work of our church.

We've looked at methods and motivation; now consider *measurement*. When I ask my daughter to carry out the garbage or wash the dishes she generally does it. Melodie learned many years ago that I would check to see if the wastebasket was empty or the dishes clean. Does God measure my evangelistic service for Him? Yes, He does. The Parable of the Talents in Matthew 25 indicates the importance of what we do with what we have. That is why we studied spiritual gifts before discussing how God expects us to use that spiritual tool kit to accomplish His work in our world.

God wants a return on His investment in us. He gave the life of His Son on the cross to save us, and sent His Spirit to abide within us to qualify us to do His work. According to Luke 19:10, "The Son of man came to seek and to save what was lost." That is now our task, through the power *He* has given. Don't get sidetracked with the argument that quality is more important than quantity. We're not looking for *either-or*, but *both-and*. God's pattern for His church is to present Jesus Christ as Saviour and Lord, lead people to receive Him, and guide them in growing as His disciples in the church.

Application

You can become the catalyst in mobilizing your whole church for evangelism. You can become the spiritual eyes and ears of the church in your community. Driving to work today, I had to turn the car's headlights on. The fog was so thick I found it difficult to see more than fifty feet ahead. Had the fog lasted all day, it would have brought blessed relief from a week of 90-degree temperatures. But by 10 o'clock the sun had burned through the fog and haze, and the temperature was up to 90 by noon. A similar spiritual fog may exist among your church members when looking at your community. It may appear that everybody is a member of a church and there is little chance for growth. Search for the facts. They have a way of burning away the fog. You will discover people around you who need to know Jesus Christ personally.

A conductor on a train in the Chicago area was retiring after forty years of service. At the retirement party he said, "It seems as if I've spent all my life trying to help people get home—and I've enjoyed every minute of it." Your church is called to do that: Help people in your community make it home to their Heavenly Father, through faith in Jesus Christ as Saviour and Lord. Once you really get involved, you'll have a sense of joy, excitement, and well-being because you'll be in step with God in fulfilling His greatest desire for His world.

6

A hot time in the city

God's love continues to touch towns and cities. How many will be reached for Christ today?

Acts 2:36-47

[36]"Therefore let all Israel be assured of this: God has made this Jesus, whom you crucified, both Lord and Christ."

[37]When the people heard this, they were cut to the heart and said to Peter and the other apostles, "Brothers, what shall we do?"

[38]Peter replied, "Repent and be baptized, every one of you, in the name of Jesus Christ so that your sins may be forgiven. And you will receive the gift of the Holy Spirit. [39]The promise is for you and your children and for all who are far off—for all whom the Lord our God will call."

[40]With many other words he warned them; and he pleaded with them, "Save yourselves from this corrupt generation." [41]Those who accepted his message were baptized, and about 3,000 were added to their number that day.

[42]They devoted themselves to the apostles' teaching and to the fellowship, to the breaking of bread and to prayer. [43]Everyone was filled with awe, and many wonders and miraculous signs were done by the apostles. [44]All the believers were together and had everything in common. [45]Selling their possessions and goods, they gave to anyone as he had need. [46]Every day they continued to meet together in the temple courts. They broke bread in their homes and ate together with glad and sincere hearts, [47]praising God and enjoying the favor of all the people. And the Lord added to their number daily those who were being saved.

In the summer of 1980 our nation went through a prolonged heat wave. Over 1,100 persons died from it. Duke Power Company set new records in our county for the kilowatt output of electricity. One night a local TV station did a feature on how businessmen in Charlotte dress in the summer. We were entertained with views of downtown at lunch hour. Women workers walked past in light, sleeveless dresses, while most of the men were wearing ties and suit coats. The simple point was that if businessmen would relax the dress code, air conditioners in offices could be set higher to conserve energy.

For several successive nights the 6 o'clock news showed the executive officers of our two leading banks walking to the prestigious City Club for lunch. As always, they had on ties and coats. No amount of joshing by the press could change their traditional dress nor get the City Club to drop the requirement of ties and coats in order to enter. One reporter quipped that it would make a real commotion in Charlotte if these two bankers were to break with tradition. He expected hundreds of other men would follow the example of those two. Needless to say, there was no commotion in Charlotte, and most businessmen wore ties and coats all summer as usual.

Two thousand years ago it was business as usual in Jerusalem. Oh, several weeks before there had been a little flurry of activity. Some Nazarene who claimed to be the Messiah was tried and crucified. Other false messiahs had made their presence known before, but there was something different about this One. He spoke with an authority the others lacked, and even the rulers said that they could find no reason to condemn Him. The noisy crowd got their way though, and He was crucified. Would you believe—some of His followers got so worked up that they reported His resurrection three days later and that He visited with them on several occasions? But, of course, things like that just don't happen.

Let's assume you are watching the 6 o'clock news. As you turn the dial, the announcer is saying, "Today, there is a commotion in Jerusalem. A report has just been received that the annual Pentecost celebration, which has been brought to Jerusalem Jews from all over the world, has been interrupted by a strange phenomenon. A group of Galileans are talking in languages understood by all these foreign visitors. We will bring further details on the late-night news."

You know the rest of the story. Peter took advantage of the situation to preach Christ to the multitudes. Yes, this is the same Peter who denied Christ earlier when asked by a slave girl if he knew Christ. Although it isn't quite the same Peter either, for he has recently had a meal and a personal commissioning from the risen Christ. This experience really transformed him. Using passages from Joel and the Psalms, he preached a mighty sermon regarding the need for salvation from sin. Before he could give an invitation, the crowd asked how to be saved.

Bible Base

Read Acts 2:36-47. Peter's sermon ends with the assurance that God has made Jesus both Lord and Christ. We use those terms pretty loosely, but they have specific meanings, which would have been clear to the audience on that Pentecost Day. *Lord* means Ruler of all things, King over all. All authority and power takes its direction and limitation from Him. *Christ* means Messiah, the promised Deliverer, the only hope the human race has ever had.

Verses 37-39 show an electrifying response to the first preaching service of the Christian church. The message had been so clear and delivered with such conviction and power from the Holy Spirit that many of the hearers blurted out, "Brothers, what shall we do?" A lot of street-corner prophets had spoken to Jerusalem's residents over the years. People would listen, then walk away when the address was over. Nothing happened. What was the difference now?

The answer to the question from the crowd is a classic statement relating to becoming a Christian. Ray Stedman decribes it: "There are two things you need to do, Peter says.... First you need to *repent*—a word which is greatly misunderstood. Feeling sorry and crying may go along with repentance, but such emotions do not necessarily mean that you have repented. To repent (Greek *metanoia*) means to change your mind. You have been thinking that everything was all right with you, but now you must think again.... The second thing to do is to be baptized. Baptism does not make you magically clean, but it is the outward and symbolic declaration of the change of mind that you have experienced inside. Baptism is an open identification with Jesus Christ."

Occasionally, I drive through a small town in eastern Pennsylvania. Main Street is about two miles long, and there are four bakeries spread along that stretch. The first one has a sign, "The Best Doughnuts in America." The next one's sign says, "The Best Doughnuts in the World," and the sign on the third one says, "The Best Doughnuts in the Universe." I always stop at the fourth bakery. Its sign says, "The Best Doughnuts on This Street!" Peter on the Day of Pentecost had the best message *ever* preached on the street where all of humanity lives. It dealt with our real need, was delivered under the guidance of the Spirit, and brought the results God intended.

Imagine the impact on Jerusalem when in just one day the

Christian church comes into being with 3,000 members! Verses 41-47 inform us that the Holy Spirit got them started immediately in a lifestyle that would assure a healthy, thriving fellowship. Four basic ingredients for a church are stated:

Baptism. Peter had just explained that baptism was the way to publicly indicate that you repented and were identifying yourself with Christ. What a service that must have been as 3,000 were baptized!

Teaching. Some people are governed primarily by experience, the guidance they receive from their emotions. But Christianity is based on solid evidence, the authoritative Word of God. Christ's disciples are to receive the Word of God and allow experience to be interpreted by it. The Scriptures and teachings of Christ were explained to these new Jerusalem converts by the Apostles. At a recent Christian college commencement, Dr. Paul Toms stated that when Christians come together they sit under the judgment of the Word. That is why solid scriptural teaching formed a foundation stone for this infant church at Jerusalem.

Fellowship. Verses 44 and 45 give a sobering illustration of the depth of fellowship shared by those Christians. Here is clear evidence of the dramatic change Christ makes in a person's life when this level of community is achieved: they shared material goods as one large family. During a revival I conducted a few years ago, this was really brought home to me. An elderly, crippled woman was at the service every night with the assistance of a younger woman. I just assumed they were mother and daughter. Near the end of the week I had lunch with the older woman. I inquired about her daughter, and she said she had none. The younger woman had been converted about a year ago. She had assisted the deaconesses once in visiting shut-ins and in so doing had met this elderly woman. As a sister in Christ she began coming every Saturday to wash the woman's hair, then she returned on Sunday mornings to bring her to worship. This fellowship had brought spiritual growth to both women.

Worship. These new Christians met daily for worship

breaking bread and praying together. How meaningful communion must have been to them. They had just experienced what it symbolized, the life and death of Christ to bring new life to others. And they prayed together. It was refreshing for the Apostles to hear the prayers of these new converts. They did not have formalized prayers printed on little cards saying, "God is great; God is good. And we thank Him for this food. By His hands we all are fed; Give us, Lord, our daily bread." No, their prayers came from hearts overflowing with joy for their newfound salvation. In the breaking of bread and in praying together, we affirm our relationship to God.

Implication

Why is there no mention of evangelism in the life of the early church? Was evangelism not being done? Verse 47 assures us that the Lord was adding to their number daily those who were being saved. When these Christians came together on the temple porch or in homes, it was with the purpose of praising God and strengthening each other. They came to learn, to worship, to pray, to fellowship. Non-Christians usually would not want to be present. The church certainly was evangelistic, though. Those saints went where non-Christians were to do their evangelizing: in the synagogues, on street corners, and in homes that were open to them. Their witness to the Gospel was not chained inside a building of wood or stone but was unleashed where it could do some good—in the world of lost men and women. The reaction to the early disciples was strong and positive. The surrounding residents were baffled at what was happening before their eyes: the Galileans speaking various languages, the changes in behavior and speech on the part of those who were converted, and the extreme closeness and unselfishness demonstrated by the Christians. These things just didn't happen every day, at least until that day. Fear of the unknown and the fear of God are often in the hearts of unbelievers when God's people are obedient to Him.

In the great Welsh revivals, fear of God was felt in a mighty way. The mules that hauled the coal carts up out of the mines had to be retaught commands. So many of the foul-mouthed miners were converted and cleaned up their language that the animals didn't recognize the commands when given without the customary oaths. Whole communities became so fearful of a God who could bring about this change that mass conversions were reported. Barrooms and dance halls were closed for lack of customers. The police force had very little work to do. Where Christians take their faith and their Master's commands seriously today, similar results are seen.

Application

The commotion that started in Jerusalem continues to touch cities and towns all over the world. How many people on this planet do you think will receive Christ today? How many will become Christians this week? Nearly 6,000 people receive Christ as Saviour daily! How many new congregations will be organized in the next month: 500? 1,000? 3,000? No. Over 6,000 new churches will come into being worldwide in the next thirty days! Much of this growth is outside North America. But just as Elijah, after the long drought, reported that he saw a cloud the size of a man's hand on the horizon, so we are seeing positive signs. Christians in America are gearing up for a new emphasis on outreach to their unsaved neighbors and associates.

Pastors and lay leaders are attending seminars to learn effective ways of sharing Christ and meeting people out in the world with the Gospel rather than expecting the lost to come to the church building for the message. A dozen or more home Bible studies in the Melrose, Massachussetts area provide neutral places where the unchurched can be invited to discuss the Bible. Churches are seeing members added by conversion as a result. Community Church in Ogden, North Carolina has a booth at the county fair. The church provides chairs in the shade so people can stop and rest. Church members give a cup of cold water in Jesus' name along with a Scripture portion. The plan of salvation is shared with all who are interested. Really, the only limit to starting the Jerusalem-church kind of commotion in your area is the limitation of your thinking.

Where are the people in your community who are most in need of the Gospel? How can you and your class gain their attention? The Lord may not astound your community pagans with a gift of tongues among you as He did in Jerusalem. He'll probably allow you to use your reasoning powers to determine a suitable plan.

A church in Minneapolis discovered most of the unsaved in its target area attended the hockey games. Here's how they started their commotion in Minneapolis: between periods at the game, beer and cigarette ads were flashed on the ice with the use of a 35mm projector. The church bought several 60-second slots of time between those ads and flashed slides with such captions as: "Jesus Saves!" "Did you know that God's last name is not Dammit?" "We are working to beat the devil." "Even in the age of inflation, the wages of sin remain the same."

Perhaps this is not the right approach to reach your community and gain attention and respect for the Gospel. But there *is* a right approach for your town. What is it? When you find it, use it for Christ. This would be a good time to discuss strategy with others in your church. Look again at the four ingredients of a functioning, New Testament church (mentioned earlier in this chapter). How do they relate to your church?

Today you have studied a model for a church, Acts 2:41-47. This outline may help you visualize how the church grows:

1. *Growing up:* Christians became better Christians (v. 42).

2. *Growing together:* They were committed to each other in the body (v. 44).

3. *Growing out:* They remained in touch with the lost around them (v. 47a).

4. *Growing more:* New people being saved was a normal thing (v. 47b).

7

Was Philip for real?

The gods of this world are materialism, cults, and humanistic philosophies, but the Christian's hope lies in the only true and unchanging God.

Acts 8:26-38

[26] Now an angel of the Lord said to Philip, "Go south to the road—the desert road—that goes down from Jerusalem to Gaza." [27] So he started out, and on his way he met an Ethiopian eunuch, an important official in charge of all the treasury of Candace, queen of the Ethiopians. This man had gone to Jerusalem to worship, [28] and on his way home was sitting in his chariot reading the Book of Isaiah the prophet. [29] The Spirit told Philip, "Go to that chariot and stay near it."

[30] Then Philip ran up to the chariot and heard the man reading Isaiah the prophet. "Do you understand what you are reading?" Philip asked.

[31] "How can I," he said, "unless someone explains it to me?" So he invited Philip to come up and sit with him.

[32] The eunuch was reading this passage of Scripture:

"He was led like a sheep to the slaughter,
and as a lamb before the shearer is silent,
so He did not open His mouth.
[33] In His humiliation He was deprived of justice.
Who can speak of His descendants?
For His life was taken from the earth."

[34] The eunuch asked Philip, "Tell me, please, who is the prophet talking about, himself or someone else?" [35] Then Philip began with that very passage of Scripture and told him the Good News about Jesus.

[36] As they traveled along the road, they came to some water and the eunuch said, "Look, here is water. Why shouldn't I be baptized?" [38] And he ordered the chariot to stop. Then both Philip and the eunuch went down into the water and Philip baptized him.

The passage of time changes our perspective on things. An older friend of mine continually talks about wishing he could be back in the Good Old Days, when coffee was a nickel and you could buy a new Ford for $495. Dan declares he actually bought a 1912 Model T for that price. The cheap prices stand out in his mind. But as we read the history of the first 25 years of this century, some other facts surface, facts Dan has conveniently forgotten.

What about the winter nights when all the quilts available couldn't keep you warm because there was no heat in the bedrooms? How about the arduous task of chopping wood after school each day for the kitchen stove? Dad worked for $20 a week, and the highlight of the week was Saturday when he got his 5¢ allowance. The tires on that Model T were forever going flat; you sprained your wrist and broke ribs trying to crank the thing in cold weather. Well, you get the picture. Those days were old, but they weren't any better than the days we live in now.

We have a tendency to look back at the early church as seen through the eyes of the New Testament and refer to that as the Good Old Days of the church. The implication is that it was easier to witness, easier to gain an audience; everyone was just waiting for an invitation to receive Christ. But the oppression of Roman rule, the worship of many pagan gods and goddesses, the skeptical attitude toward anything new made it seem humanly impossible for Christianity to gain a foothold. Still, there is no denying the air of excitement then. That excitement does not always exist in the twentieth-century church. We face materialism, cults, and humanism as well. But we have the same God and a much richer heritage on which to build our ministries: 2,000 years of witness to Christ as Saviour and Lord, groups of believers in most cities and towns, meeting places where we can gather for praise, prayer, and instruction. Add to that the printed word, radio, TV, and all the media available for making Christ known. No, I don't wish for an opportunity to serve Christ in the first century. I'm quite satisfied to be on hand in the exciting world of the 1980s.

Sometimes we hesitate to really get involved in making disciples because we fear we won't do it perfectly like the first-century Christians did. God's purpose in providing us with the Scriptures was basically to reveal Himself and His plan for our redemption. He saw to it that enough related material was included so we could see that the Old and New Testament saints were not perfect people on pedestals. They made mistakes and had their failures. It did not stop them. Peter denied Christ three times but later went on to preach that dynamic message on the Day of Pentecost when 3,000 were converted. Yes, Peter was for real.

Perhaps you have attempted some things for God in the past and failed. Don't fear that if you try again you'll have another failure; rather, fear that if you don't try again you'll miss the blessing of succeeding in some ministry for Christ. The early Christians were real people; they had wins and losses. A key to their spiritual growth and usefulness in Christ's work was not how many times they did some good deed but rather their ability to continue in spite of occasional failures. Remember, Babe Ruth struck out three times for every home run he hit.

Bible Base

Read Acts 8:26-38. The time frame is about four years after Pentecost. There were probably over 10,000 Christians. The church had just experienced its first serious persecution. Until then the religious leaders had occasionally given them a hard time, but the Christians had been pretty comfortable in Jerusalem. They had taken the first step of Acts 1:8, witnessing for Christ in Jerusalem, but had done nothing with the rest of the verse, "in all Judea and Samaria, and to the ends of the earth." Christ had to do some nudging to get His church reaching out beyond home base. The persecution succeeded in doing that by scattering the believers throughout Judea and Samaria. The first part of Acts 8 records this and Philip's ministry to Samaria. As he used his gift of evangelism, the Lord blessed and Samaritans came to Christ.

Philip was for real. He was not particularly any better than the other disciples. What stands out was his availability and usability. He's a good model for twentieth-century disciples who want to be used of God.

The key to usability is not so much "ability" as it is "availability." It was true when Christ was on earth; it remains true today: He uses only those who are available, cleansed, put right. Could we, would we, become the available people—now, today, through rightness with Him?

This incident with the Ethiopian has four parts. First, verses 27, 29, and 30 show Philip to be open to God's leading. After what had been happening in Samaria, I'm afraid I'd have given the Lord an argument when He asked me to leave an area where I was reaching many people for Christ and go down on the Gaza Road. That would be like leaving a teeming city like Los Angeles to go to Death Valley. Just imagine how long it would take to walk the 80 miles. But there was no hesitation: "So he started out."

The wisdom of following God's leading became evident. Along the Gaza Road came an Ethiopian eunuch, treasurer to the queen of Ethiopia. This Gentile official had been to Jerusalem. On his way home he was reading from the Book of Isaiah. A man of his bearing wouldn't be traveling alone. His chariot was probably attended by guards and servants. The custom of the day was to read aloud. Imagine Philip's surprise when he heard this person reading from Isaiah 53, about the Suffering Servant. Now he understood why God had sent him to the desert. The Spirit told him to go near to the chariot and stay with it. "Stay near it" is translated from the Greek word for *collage,* meaning glue or cement. "Glue yourself to that chariot, Philip."

The second insight on this passage is that Philip had a knowledge of the Scriptures (vv. 31-35). He was able to recognize what the man was reading. When Philip asked, "Do you understand what you are reading?" it may have been asked in surprise. But it was the opening needed to share the Gospel, since the man invited him into the chariot to explain the passage.

Sometimes we do not encourage converts to get involved in witnessing because they don't yet have a grasp of the Scriptures. That understanding is indeed necessary to effectively lead people into a firm relationship with Jesus Christ. The foundation for this kind of instruction, though, is laid by persons who can share at the experience level. Remember the blind man in John 9 who was asked what he knew about the Man who had restored his sight. The answer was simply, "One thing I do know. I was blind but now I see! ... If this Man were not from God, He could do nothing" (John 9:25, 33).

Not long after his conversion, Barry Lyon of Oak Hill Bible Church in Oxford, Massachusetts had opportunity to share with Gary Russell, a close friend. He was not able to give a Bible discourse but just shared what changes Christ had made in his life. It caught Gary's interest, and he and his wife, Debbie, then sought spiritual counsel from the pastor and other more mature Christians. That combination brought both Gary and Debbie to accept Christ. Are you a new Christian? Share faithfully what Christ is doing in your life. And take advantage of opportunities to learn God's Word so you can also lead people to understand God's plan for salvation and new life.

Philip obviously knew how to relate to people. This third insight comes from the way he handled the initial contact with the Ethiopian. Several times prior to this we've seen Philip in action. He was one of those chosen to handle the problem of care for widows in Jerusalem who had no family nearby. And he performed admirably in Samaria ministering with those half-Jews who were usually despised by full-blooded Jews. When any Christian is willing to be used by God, the Lord continually prepares that person for effective ministry. You may have heard the Gospel several times before committing your life to Christ. But think about the person who made the greatest impression on you in that process. What was it about his or her approach that impressed you and caused you to respond? That may be a clue for you in relating effectively with non-Christian neighbors.

Acts 8:36-38 give a fourth insight. Philip expected a decision. Robert Schuller would call him a Possibility Thinker. He was an optimist, assuming that God would honor His Word and Philip's witness, and the result would be a firm decision for Christ. Part of Philip's witness to the Good News about Jesus was pointing out that baptism is a symbol of the change in our lives when we take Christ as our Saviour. It is publicly acknowledging Christ as Lord. Philip witnessed, the Ethiopian was sensitive to the message, the Holy Spirit worked in his heart, and he received Christ. As they passed some water by the road, the new convert decided to seal his decision and requested that Philip baptize him. Imagine the scene: Here is this influential Ethiopian official being baptized while all his caravan stands by to observe. I wonder what was going through their minds.

Perhaps the official passed on to his group the things he had learned from Philip. A contemporary chorus puts it well: "It only takes a spark to get a fire going, and soon all those around will warm up to its glowing." Scholars think this man may have been the key missionary to Ethiopia. At any rate, there was a growing Christian church there by the end of the first century.

Implication

This passage teaches some principles about personal witnessing:

1. Be open to the leading of the Holy Spirit (vv. 26, 29).
2. Prompt obedience to God's guidance is necessary (vv. 27a, 30a)
3. God provides contacts with seeking people.
4. Recognize people's needs, and seek to meet them (v. 30).
5. Know Scripture; be able to present Christ tactfully.

What other lessons might be added to this list?

I was impressed with the barriers Philip had to overcome in his own background. As a Jew he had been brought up to believe that the Jews were a superior race. There was to be no close involvement with Gentiles, a classification given to all non-Jews. In order to share Christ with the Ethiopian, Philip had to approach the man before he could have known whether he was a Jew. (Verse 27 says he had been to Jerusalem to worship, but whether he was a proselyte or just curious is not known.) We have our cultural prejudices too, tending to shun persons of a certain nationality or racial or socio-economic background. These marks of culture *do* divide people who are apart from Christ. Don't overlook that in your witnessing. However, in Christ the differences fade away. For the Christian there are only two classes of people: the saved and the lost. My great-uncle Fred used to amaze and amuse me with some of his little ditties. One of them went like this:

It's hard to tell
The depth of the well
By the length of the handle on the pump.

Non-Christians allow the length of the handle on the pump to affect their choice of friends and associates. Christians allow

Christ to help them ignore the outward appearances, or the length of the handle. Instead, we try to make sure the well is deep enough so the person can find Christ.

If you and I are to enjoy witnessing opportunities such as Philip had, we'll have to take our witness out from behind the walls of our church building into our neighborhoods. The boys' choir in a fashionable city church was going to sing "Onward Christian Soldiers" for the processional in the Sunday morning service. After the Saturday rehearsal, several of the boys had an idea. They would make some crosses to carry down the aisle as they sang. Out came hammers and nails, and soon twelve crosses were made. They could hardly wait to dramatize their song. The next morning the choir director was horrified at what he saw. "You can't do this, boys. Put the crosses behind the door!" But the boys had their revenge. You can just see the director's face as they marched down the aisle singing:

> Onward Christian soldiers,
> Marching as to war,
> With the cross of Jesus
> Hid behind the door.

I wonder how many of us left the cross of Jesus hidden behind the door this week as we went to work or school or picnicked with neighbors? Life's greatest satisfactions are found as we witness to what Christ is doing in our lives while we engage in the normal activities of the day. Peter's counsel is, "Always be prepared to give an answer to everyone who asks you to give the reason for the hope that you have" (1 Peter 3:15). How would you state the reasons *you* have for hope in Christ? Put this in language that a person without church background can understand.

Application
In introducing his translation of the Book of Acts, J.B. Phillips says, "These men did not make acts of faith, they believed;

did not say their prayers, they really prayed. They didn't hold conferences on psychosomatic medicine, they simply healed the sick. . . . But if they were uncomplicated by modern standards, we have ruefully to admit they were open on the Godward side in a way that is almost unknown today. Consequently, it is a matter of sober history that never before have any small body of ordinary people so moved the world that their enemies could say that these men 'have turned the world upside down.' "[1]

Acts 8 illustrates our definition of evangelism:

1. Evangelism is the *communication* of the Good News that Jesus Christ died for our sins and was raised from the dead; and that, as the living Lord, He offers forgiveness of sins and the gift of the Holy Spirit to all who believe and repent.

2. Evangelism seeks a *response* from people to become reconciled to God through Jesus Christ.

3. Evangelism *anticipates* an obedience to our Lord, maturing in the faith, and responsible service within His church and through His church.

Adrian Shepard explains it this way: "Evangelism means that we:

a. Accept ourselves as chosen of God for service.
b. Accept ourselves as fruit bearers for our Lord.
c. Accept the burden of our Lord for persons who are lost.
d. Accept ourselves as lovers for our Lord seeking to find ways to reach those outside of fellowship with God."[2]

As you think about evangelism in your community, the task may at first seem overwhelming. Where do I start? Can I get people to listen? Should I just quote six verses of Scripture?

There are three ingredients which make up New Testament evangelism. The first is *Presence*. Usually this helps us make initial contacts with pagans around us. Presence evangelism involves discovering needs in the lives of people and developing ministries to meet those needs. It is an application of the formula, "Find a need and fill it; find a hurt and heal it." Some churches discover Presence ministries meaning for them things like a weekly mother's-day-out (baby-sitting provided at the church), clothing closet, tutoring for children, or counseling for troubled families. The result of Presence evangelism is that people are helped.

Next is the ingredient of *Proclamation.* Once we have gained a hearing with people, we need to communicate the Gospel so people will understand that Christ died for their sins, that He can make them free from the guilt and penalty of sin, that He provides "belonging" through His church, and that He offers the kingdom to those who trust and obey Him. Every Christian is called to follow the example of early Christians who "preached the Word wherever they went" (Acts 8:4). Often we rely on the Sunday School teacher and preacher to do this for us.

A third ingredient of New Testament evangelism is *Persuasion.* For a long time we've shied away from that concept, thinking it unspiritual. While it is true that the Holy Spirit leads people to receive Christ, He generally uses a human being as an instrument. Dr. Donald McGavran refers to a theology of harvest: If God's Word is faithfully proclaimed, a harvest *will* result. People *will* be saved. We'll know it has happened because our church *will* experience a measurable increase. Persuasion evangelism not only brings people to Christ, but also brings them into responsible church membership where they can mature in Christ.

8

Ephesian epidemic

What are churches used for — worship or tourism?

Acts 19:23-29

²³About that time there arose a great disturbance about the Way. ²⁴A silversmith named Demetrius, who made silver shrines of Artemis, brought in no little business for the craftsmen. ²⁵He called them together, along with the workmen in related trades, and said: "Men, you know we receive a good income from this business. ²⁶And you see and hear how this fellow Paul has convinced and led astray large numbers of people here in Ephesus and in practically the whole province of Asia. He says that man-made gods are no gods at all. ²⁷There is danger not only that our trade will lose its good name, but also that the temple of the great goddess Artemis will be discredited, and the goddess herself, who is worshiped throughout the province of Asia and the world, will be robbed of her divine majesty."

²⁸When they heard this, they were furious and began shouting: "Great is Artemis of the Ephesians!" ²⁹Soon the whole city was in an uproar.

Acts 20:28-31

²⁸Guard yourselves and all the flock of which the Holy Spirit has made you overseers. Be shepherds of the church of God, which He bought with His own blood. ²⁹I know that after I leave, savage wolves will come in among you and will not spare the flock. ³⁰Even from your own number men will arise and distort the truth in order to draw away disciples after them. ³¹So be on your guard!

Revelation 2:4-5

⁴Yet I hold this against you: You have forsaken your first love. ⁵Remember the height from which you have fallen! Repent and do the things you did at first. If you do not repent, I will come to you and remove your lampstand from its place.

The year 1933 is important to me. That's the year I was born. It is also the year that The City of Tomorrow exhibit caused such a great stir at the Chicago World's Fair. Architects, planners, and designers had created in miniature a display of what they thought the city of the future would look like. Some of our rapidly expanding metropolises are surprisingly similar to that design. Skyscrapers with heliports on top, multilevel, six-lane highways, moving sidewalks to get people around efficiently, and totally enclosed city centers with a controlled atmosphere were some of the features. You'll find these things today in Minneapolis, Charlotte, Los Angeles. After people had viewed the exhibit for about six months, someone noticed that The City of Tomorrow had no churches. When asked for the reason, the display coordinator replied, "We did not think there would be any need for churches in the city of the future!" Christians have recognized the need for churches for nearly 2,000 years. But more and more the world is not aware of this need.

Can you glibly assume that your church will always exist? Dr. William Steuart McBirnie, professor of Middle East Studies at California Graduate School of Theology, thinks not: "There is no predestined certainty that the church will survive the next half century. Those who quote 'The gates of hell shall not prevail against it' (Matt. 16:18, KJV) as the guarantee that the church cannot fail, are missing the illustration. Gates belong to a city, a fortress, a castle. As long as the church is *on the march*, taking the initiative, storming the gates even of hell itself, nothing can stand before it. The gates of hell will neither stand nor prevail, but will fall before the onslaught.

"But the church that stays in camp will never break down the doors of the citadel of sin. God says that such churches cannot become victorious, and indeed are doomed to death. To the church at Sardis, Jesus said: 'Thou hast a name that thou livest, and art dead!' "¹ (Rev. 3:1, KJV)

When churches make a habit of staying in camp, the world sees no need of including them in modern society. I saw a church that remained in camp when I visited Saint Paul's Cathedral in London. The original building was destroyed by the Fire of London in 1666. Sir Christopher Wren was commissioned to design a new cathedral. Other buildings bear his name as architect, but Saint Paul's was his masterpiece. This place for worship was once filled with thousands of people each Lord's Day. But when I visited it one Sunday morning, I found fewer than 100 worshipers, all gathered way down front in a place which could seat thousands. It was difficult to hear what the rector was saying because of the sightseers. Though few people were worshiping, hundreds were touring the perimeter of the sanctuary to view the architecture and see where some of the "greats" of England were buried in the hallways. Over the years, the membership of Saint Paul's stayed in camp rather than blanketing London with the Gospel. And, as McBirnie said, "Such churches cannot become victorious, and indeed are doomed to death."

The Apostle Paul spent three years in Ephesus while on his third missionary tour. He saw this as a key city for advancing Christ's cause. It was the political, commercial, and cultural capital of the entire province of Asia. For three months, he discussed Christ in the Jewish synagogue. Then some of the Jews realized his teaching was at odds with their legalistic interpretation of Scripture. They began speaking evil of the Gospel, so Paul rented a nearby school, the lecture hall of Tyrannus. For over two years, he taught there daily from 11 A.M. to 4 P.M. Ephesus was affected by this intensive effort. Acts 19:13-20 tells about the sincerity of hundreds who turned from witchcraft to Christ. Throughout history, whenever the Gospel has been presented with power, it has faced resistance and persecution. And the resistance was growing in Ephesus.

Bible Base

Read Acts 19:23-29. The temple of Artemis was prominent in Ephesus. It must have been quite a sight. In its day it was one of the wonders of the world. Historians say it took 220 years to build. It was 425 feet long and 220 feet wide, and 127 columns surrounded it. Artemis was the goddess of sex and fertility. Her statues contained as many as 100 breasts. Every May people from all over Asia came for festive celebrations at Ephesus. Apparently the riot described here took place at the annual celebration in A.D.47

The turmoil at Ephesus points up that the Gospel of Christ is at enmity with all other faiths and religions. It can't be Jesus and Artemis, or Jesus and astrology, or Jesus and anything else. Christianity is not just another set of standards which affect the intellect; it is a way of life which demands total submission to Jesus Christ as Lord. A lot of people had surrendered to Christ during Paul's three years in Ephesus. It really showed up at the annual Artemis Days celebration. The silversmiths were unhappy because sales of statues of the goddess were down. Demetrius, the steward of the silversmith union, checked out the situation. All leads pointed to Paul and the followers of the Way as being responsible. This shrewd craftsman launched a threefold attack against Paul and the Christians.

First, verse 27 records the charge that they were losing money with the low sales. Then he charged that faith in Artemis would decline, and finally, that their city might lose the prestige it enjoyed by being such a great worship center. Even today nothing stirs people into a frenzy like a religious appeal based on practical business principles. The tactics of some "electronic churches" and Christian/political groups of our day are vivid illustrations.

In the 20th chapter of Acts, Paul charges the leaders of the Ephesian church to faithfulness in leading the fellowship. While exciting things had happened as these new Christians shared their faith throughout the city and area, the forces of evil were gearing up for an attack. Verses 28-31 reveal the keen insight of Paul. Satan uses two avenues to attack a church: savage wolves attack from without, and those within the church arise to distort the truth. Paul had experience with both kinds of enemy. He had seen the Judaizers come to various congregations and try to lead them into slavery to the Old Testament legalistic pattern. And, in some of his letters, he named teachers who had adopted false doctrines and led immature Christians into cultic practices.

Therefore, the church in every age must build on the firm foundation of Scripture, and constantly watch for those who misinterpret truth so that they can be guided back on course. "I never stopped warning each of you night and day with tears," Paul said to the Ephesian leaders. He poured himself out to them so they could be strong leaders. The word for "stopped" actually means shrink. It is a nautical term, meaning to take in sail. He is telling the leaders that even when it would have been easier to say nothing, he did not take in his sail but continued to confront men with the Gospel.

Now read Revelation 2:4-5. This ominous letter to the church at Ephesus was written about forty years after the events recorded in Acts 19. What had gone wrong? With Paul as founder and a strong core of leaders trained by Paul, how could this congregation in such a short time go from a bright firebrand for Christ to a stagnant group who was in danger of losing its identity as a church? The Scripture doesn't give many details. The doctrines of Balaam and the Nicolaitans were leading some congregations astray, but apparently the elders had followed Paul's counsel well since the Spirit notes that they hate the doctrines of the Nicolaitans.

Implication

What went wrong at Ephesus? Remember its position as a key city politically, commercially, and culturally. Paul also considered it a key city as an evangelistic base. Next to Antioch, Paul used this city and congregation as a base to evangelize all Asia Minor. It seems to have been the mother church for the seven congregations mentioned in Revelation 2 and 3. Evangelism was a key priority for the Ephesian church. As long as that emphasis was maintained, Ephesus was a healthy church growing in numbers and establishing new congregations. At some point this activity slowed. Perhaps the keen awareness of Acts 4:12 was no longer their watchword: "Salvation is found in no one else, for there is no other name under heaven given to men by which we must be saved."

When evangelism no longer receives priority in the ministry of a church and in the lives of each member, the natural result is a slowdown in the rate of conversions to Christ. More and more new members come by transfer of membership from another congregation rather than through evangelism and baptism. What might take the place of evangelism as a church's primary emphasis? For the past twenty-five years Protestantism has increasingly emphasized the need for sacrificial service to mankind, as called for in Matthew 22:39, "Love your neighbor as yourself." The church has tended to look at the community more in terms of its being insufficiently clothed, hungry, or oppressed rather than its being lost, separated from God, condemned.

The New Testament sets both evangelism and social concern as the church's work in the world. The Lausanne Covenant on World Evangelization puts them in this order: "In the church's mission of sacrificial service, evangelism is primary." Numerous studies of Protestant denominations over the past twenty-five years indicate a decline for those whose primary emphasis was social concern; those whose primary emphasis was evangelism increased.[2] Do we have to forget social concerns in order to win people for Christ? Not at all. The Gallup poll group recently discovered that 42 percent of the members of evangelical churches are involved in helping the poor, the sick, the handicapped, the elderly. Only 26 percent of the more liberal denominations' members are involved in social concerns.[3] The primary difference is whether one sees the meeting of social needs as a goal or as a means of reaching a goal. Non-evangelicals often have as a goal the meeting of human needs at physical and social levels more than the meeting of spiritual needs. Evangelicals are concerned with the human suffering around them and respond to those needs as a means to the goal of making disciples. An evangelical may provide food and clothing for a needy family as an opportunity to get acquainted and at the right moment share the Gospel. A nonevangelical might see only his responsibility to provide the food and clothing.

Yes, it is possible to lose the first love for Christ—that zeal and enthusiasm that drives us in the early days of being a Christian so that we want to share the Good News with everyone. A church recently completed an analysis of the past ten years of its history: membership and attendance figures, information on how new members were gained (children of church families, transfer or converts outside church families) and budget analysis. The official board discovered several signs that seemed to suggest why attendance and giving were in decline. Of the thirty new members added during the period, nineteen were children of church members, and eleven were transfers from other churches. There were no additions by conversion of people from families not associated previously with a church. The budget analysis showed that in addition to maintaining their buildings and paying the pastor's salary and expenses, they gave 10 percent to denominational causes. The only other significant expenditures were to support a community crisis-line project and contributions to Meals-on-Wheels for neighborhood shut-ins. The only item identifiable for evangelism was a one-week revival meeting two years before, which of course was attended by the faithful members. What went wrong? As long as evangelism had priority at Ephesus, the church grew. When other things took priority, the church declined. The story is repeated in this church. It can happen to any church—even your church: "You have forsaken your first love" (Rev. 2:4).

Application

Can we prevent the Ephesian Epidemic from striking our churches? Think back to the time you were converted. Try to recapture something of the freshness of life, the excitement that came through knowing you had made things right with God, the peace that came to your heart—and the desire to see everybody else have the same experience. I'll never forget John's conversion. We were living in Plainville, Connecticut. John was the furnace repairman. His children were in our Sunday School, but no one had been able to reach John for Christ. Eventually, after several furnace breakdowns brought John to the parsonage for repair work, he opened up one night and received Christ. What an instantaneous change in a man's life! He was so zealous in sharing his newfound faith that his boss had to ask him to go easy with his witnessing. He was coming on so strong that customers were being offended. Why, he even made some of us in the church a little uneasy. At prayer meeting he talked about people he had been witnessing to, while we talked about praying for Aunt Maggie's ingrown toenail.

An Ephesian Epidemic can be prevented by having a constant flow of new converts coming into the congregation. Their zeal and enthusiasm are catching; it rubs off on some of the sit-and-soak members and they get charged up again about the great truth of salvation only in Christ. One of the older saints in a Dover, New Hampshire church recently shared how much joy had come to her life in recent months. Ever since her husband died, she had been a spectator in the church. Now she was accompanying a new Christian in a weekly visitation ministry in the community. "It makes me feel so good to be needed and used," she said with tears of joy streaming down her face.

Who was the last adult convert to come into your church? What have you done to keep that person's zeal alive? New converts don't know all the rules and traditions we have built up around the Gospel over the years, and we tend to shy away from them when they break some of our rules. But one of the greatest things that can happen is for mature Christians to befriend these new converts and help them develop in the faith. You have something to offer by the example of your life, and the new Christian in return can draw you into his or her circle of zeal and excitement over the reality of being saved from sin and saved to serve Christ as Lord. What might happen if you made an appointment to meet with a new Christian this week? Think about ways to share what Christ has meant to you in the time since you became a Christian. Then ask the new convert to share what the Lord is doing in his/her experience.

The new converts in your church are vital to the health and enlargement of the church. They have contacts with many unsaved friends and relatives. We who have been Christians for several years have formed friendships with other Christians and consequently have little close fellowship with lost people. There's nothing wrong with that; it just happens. It usually takes six months or more for a new Christian to break ties with unsaved friends and develop new Christian friendship circles. While the contacts with non-Christians are still existent, you might be able to help a new Christian discover ways of sharing faith with them. That can usually be done best outside of a formal church meeting.

Dr. Win Arn, of the Institute for American Church Growth, interviewed 4,000 new Christians to learn how they first came to church. The results shed some light on the importance of our daily witness:

6-8 percent just walked in without prior contact.

2-3 percent came because of the church's programs.

8-12 percent were attracted by the pastor.
3-4 percent came because of a special need.
1-2 percent were visited by members.
3-4 percent came through a Sunday School class.
70-80 percent were invited by friends and relatives.

It is probable that two-thirds of the new Christians in your church were first introduced to Christ through friends or relatives. That means, even if you've been a Christian forty years, there are probably still some unsaved people in your sphere of influence. Make a list of these non-Christian friends and relatives. Use this list first as a prayer reminder. Then ask God to guide you in knowing how to approach some of these people with a witness for Christ. Above all, pray for God's guidance. Activity like this is an almost-sure cure for losing your first love.

Non-Christian
friends

Non-Christian
relatives

9

Testing the soil

Jesus speaks to us in ways we can understand — He knows our daily needs.

Matthew 13:3-8, 18-23

³Then He told them many things in parables, saying: "A farmer went out to sow his seed. ⁴As he was scattering the seed, some fell along the path, and the birds came and ate it up. ⁵Some fell on rocky places, where it did not have much soil. It sprang up quickly, because the soil was shallow. ⁶But when the sun came up, the plants were scorched, and they withered because they had no root. ⁷Other seed fell among thorns, which grew up and choked the plants. ⁸Still other seed fell on good soil, where it produced a crop—a hundred, sixty, or thirty times what was sown.

¹⁸"Listen then to what the Parable of the Sower means: ¹⁹When anyone hears the message about the kingdom and does not understand it, the evil one comes and snatches away what was sown in his heart. This is the seed sown along the path. ²⁰What was sown on rocky places is the man who hears the Word and at once receives it with joy. ²¹But since he has no root, he lasts only a short time. When trouble or persecution comes because of the Word, he quickly falls away. ²²What was sown among the thorns is the man who hears the Word, but the worries of this life and the deceitfulness of wealth choke it, making it unfruitful. ²³But what was sown on good soil is the man who hears the Word and understands it. He produces a crop, yielding a hundred, sixty, or thirty times what was sown."

We were Southern city slickers and the real-estate man was a shrewd Yankee businessman. I'll never forget the ride in his eighty-five horsepower Ford. He would sort of lean forward in the seat going up hills, as though he could make it easier for the underpowered engine to get us over the top. It was the early 1940s, and my parents wanted to get away from city life. This farm was a steal, according to the agent.

After three years of trying to make a living on that ninety-acre farm, the reason we were able to buy it so reasonably became evident. Under the three or four inches of topsoil was a gravel base. Hay, pasture, and the garden did well during the summer. But when roots needed to draw water and food from deep down, the gravel just couldn't meet the need. After we spent three long years of backbreaking effort, the farm was sold to a man who put it to its rightful use: he turned it into a gravel pit. Highways all over the area were eventually covered with our old farm.

Have you ever planted a garden? We've tried to offset the rising cost of food by planting some of our favorite foods: squash, cucumbers, tomatoes, beans, and okra. This summer my wife, Millie, got a great garden started. Then, when it came time to do a lot of cultivating, harvesting, and canning, she left for several weeks to teach in camps. Once again I became a farmer. But this time I was pleasantly surprised. Our vegetables were growing in red clay which she had enriched with peat moss. After the plants began growing, she added a heavy straw mulch between the rows. The straw held moisture and cut the baking effect of the hot summer sun, and the peat moss kept the clay from hardening like cement.

When Millie returned from Texas, she found that our youngest daughter and I had canned fifteen jars of pickles and twelve jars of green beans. During the rest of July and August, she was able to serve fresh vegetables for supper from the garden, and she did a lot of canning and freezing. My negative feelings toward farming that had developed as a boy had changed drastically by the end of the summer. What made the difference? Back on the farm we had given much the same care in planting the seed and cultivating that we had given the backyard garden. The summers are just as hot and dry now as they were in the '40s. But the primary difference between the two experiences was the soil.

Bible Base

Read Matthew 13:3-8, 18-23. Our Lord often used agricultural imagery in His teaching since He was dealing primarily with rural people. Effective teaching today would call for a wider variety of illustrations: computer technology, nuclear power, inflation. Jesus was a master when it came to teaching by parables—simple and common events used to convey spiritual truths. The parables were windows to help people see and understand truths that are vital to serving God acceptably. The Parable of the Sower is the first of seven parables Jesus taught on this very busy day. The Kingdom of God was the basic subject of each one. Jesus shows us that the Kingdom is not just a hope for the future; it relates to life in the present as well as life in eternity.

There are three elements in the parable. The first is the *seed*. What is the seed that the farmer scatters over the field? It is the message about the Kingdom, according to verse 19, the message Jesus proclaimed concerning Himself and His Kingdom. Our Advent Christians get excited about preaching the coming Kingdom of God. This emphasis led to our founding as an association of churches in 1860. Yet that Second-Coming emphasis is only part of the message of the Kingdom which Jesus heralded across Galilee in His public ministry and private teaching sessions with the apostles. Dr. Arthur Glasser, a professor at Fuller Theological Seminary, described it this way in a lecture I heard him give:

The Gospel of the Kingdom is the response to five great questions:

1. Who am I? I was created to have fellowship with God.

2. How can I be made fit for God's presence? I am justified by faith; Jesus Christ has atoned for my sins by His death on the cross.

3. Can my life be changed? Yes. The Christian life is one of sanctification. The Holy Spirit is constantly at work changing my character.

4. To whom do I belong? I belong to a community of God's people, the body of Christ.

5. Is there hope for this world? The Gospel of the Kingdom is the hope for this world in both the present and the future. Therefore, we preach less than the Kingdom of God if we deal only with the future judgment and home of the saints.

The second element in the parable is the *sower*. Who is it that sows the seed of the Kingdom? Obviously, Jesus was the original sower. He commits the task of spreading the Gospel of the Kingdom to all who claim Him as Saviour and Lord. That is our message today in making disciples. The Gospel is to be preached as a witness to all nations. So sowers come in all sizes and shapes and colors. Revelation 5:9, speaking about Jesus, says, "You were slain, and with Your blood You purchased men for God from every tribe and language and people and nation." The only requirement is that we have been purchased for God through Christ's shed blood. When we become Christians, we automatically become responsible for sowing the Gospel. That's why we are called to be good stewards of the Gospel and are reminded that trustees are expected to be faithful with what is entrusted to them.

The final element is the *soil*. This is really the only variable in the parable. Four kinds are mentioned and later described. The parched path represents the person who makes no response to the Gospel witness. The rocky places symbolize one who makes an initial emotional response but does not follow through with commitment to Christ. Thorny soil signifies the person who tries to receive Christ without giving up his other gods of possession and prestige. And the good soil is the one who hears, understands, and responds to the Gospel in such a way that is shows in a changed life. You can probably think of acquaintances who fit each of these descriptions.

Implication

As Jesus ministered to rural people of His day, He carefully chose His illustrations. In a farm setting, sowing is done in anticipation of reaping a harvest. In Matthew 9 He talked about mankind as a field ready to be harvested, and challenged His disciples with the opportunity of reaping that harvest. They knew what He meant.

The last time I was in Alton, New York I stopped to see Homer Collins, a Christian friend. It was harvesttime, and Homer was out in his apple orchards. The combination of rain and sun had been just right, and he had an abundant crop. As I watched the pickers, I noted that not all the apples on each tree were picked. Experienced men and women knew which ones were ripe and those were picked. The others would need more time to reach the proper degree of sweetness and color. Perhaps workers would eventually pick each tree several times.

If human beings can be perceptive enough to know how to get the best harvest from an orchard, shouldn't we also expect that Christians can be sensitive enough to bring in an abundant harvest of converts for Jesus Christ? Just as all the apples weren't ripe at once, not everyone in your community or where you work will be ready to receive Christ today. That's why the harvesting technique of scaring people into the kingdom with the threat of hellfire usually isn't too effective. While sociologists can't give us all the reasons for it, in many communities there are whole blocks or groups of people who are not open to the Gospel. On foreign mission fields these are usually called resistant people. Can you think of some resistant groups in your community? The group may be definable by economic class, educational level, racial or language similarity. How much evangelistic effort should your church invest in this resistant group?

There are ways to identify whether people are ready to be challenged to repent of sin and receive Christ as Saviour. This comes through getting to know men and women well enough to discover where they are in their understanding of the Gospel. James Engel and H. Wilbert Norton deal with this in their book, *What's Gone Wrong with the Harvest?* Here's a summary of their presentation:

Level one—Ignorant of Jesus Christ, pays no attention to the Gospel.

Level two—Aware of Jesus Christ, sees Christ as one of several options.

Level three—Understands the Gospel, realizes what salvation means.

Level four—Becomes personally involved with Christ, realizes the changes Christ could make in his life.

Level five—Makes a decision for or against receiving Christ.

Level six—Receives Christ, becomes a disciple.

Obviously our goal is to see people come to level six, so that as new Christians they can then begin to grow in grace and help reach others for Christ. A person at level one won't accept Christ when you extend the invitation. The point made by Engel and Norton is that wherever a person is on the scale, your task is to bring him or her through each level until level five is reached. Then you present the plan of salvation and encourage the praying of a prayer of confession and acceptance of Christ by faith.

Think of members of your immediate family who may not be Christians. At what level is each one? At what level have you been aiming your witness? The discovery I made was that I usually treated everyone as a level-four person. Yet I have some friends and kinfolk who are still back at level two, with only a hazy idea of who Christ is and what the Gospel is all about. I'm asking God to help me revise my strategies to become more effective with those persons.

The impression you get in reading all the agricultural illustrations Jesus used is that God is pleased when a harvest is reaped. In the Parable of the Fig Tree in Luke 13 we the Lord says that the soil around a barren tree should be loosened up and a good dose of fertilizer worked in to try to get it to produce figs (v. 8). And the conclusion is, "If it bears fruit next year, fine!" (v. 9) In another agricultural picture, that of raising sheep, Dr. Donald McGavran puts it this way: "It is not enough to search for lost sheep. The Master Shepherd is not pleased with a token search; He wants His sheep found. The purpose is not to search, but to find. The goal is not to send powdered milk or kind messages to the son in the far country. It is to see him walking through the front door of his Father's house."[1]

Remember my care of my wife's garden during the summer? Millie was surprised when she arrived home and found I had taken good care of it, tended to the bean vines as she had, coaxed the summer squash, and canned some pickles. But she was also pleased and proud that her garden had provided such a good harvest. When you and I allow God's Spirit to use us in bringing persons into His family, He is very pleased with that harvest too.

Application

Most Bibles caption Matthew 13 as the Parable of the Sower, picking up on verse 18. Perhaps now you'll think of it as the Parable of the Soils, because it makes us aware of the different responses our witness for Christ may bring. Since God expects us to reap a good harvest of men and women, boys and girls into His kingdom through our church, we should explore ways of discovering good soil. A time-tested axiom is that you cannot safely take a person any farther down the road than you have gone yourself. I learned the importance of that when I assisted Director Ron Thomas at Camp Suwanee. We were developing a ten-day canoe trip through the Okefenokee Swamp and down the Suwanee River. Ron applied the axiom when he gathered all of us who were to be staff and made an early spring run so there would be no surprises when we took teens through during the summer. The staff run was the last week of March, and the swamp was not open for canoeing until April 1. We had to begin the trip just below the swamp. That following summer with the teens we did have several surprises, one very scary, on the swamp section of the trip. But on the Suwanee River everything went smoothly.

How might you apply this to the Parable of the Soils? Think in terms of your own life as well as your community. What is your personal receptivity level to the Gospel? Check it out on this chart.

Personal Soil Testing

Types	My definition	Examples in my life	Ways to improve my soil
hard path			
rocky places			
thorny soil			
good soil			

As the seed of God's Word continues to grow in my own life, I become more useful to God as an instrument for spiritual harvest in His world. Jesus said He came to save that which was lost. He trained twelve men to carry on that work after His ascension to heaven. For nearly 2,000 years this ministry has been passed on from one generation of Christians to another. When you get right down to the facts, the church is always just one generation away from extinction. God has not revealed a Plan B to put into effect if you and I don't get involved in harvest. Kind of scary, isn't it? But it is also exciting to realize that you're on the same team with the God of the universe, and while your strength and ability may be weak, your Partner has more than enough for both of you.

Along with testing the soil of your own heart, it will be helpful to test the soil around your church and in the community where you live. This chart may be useful when applied to your church community as well as to the non-Christians in your friendship circle and among your relatives.

Community Soil Testing

Types	People or groups	How to improve the soil
hard path		
rocky places		
thorny soil		
good soil		

Refer back to the six levels listed earlier in the chapter for some help with the soil-improvement column above. You will need to be creative here, and you can be. God will guide you.

We are told in Psalm 32:8-9 that one must lead a horse with a bit in its mouth, but God wants to lead you through thoughts to your mind. What ideas for harvest has He given you?

There are several signs to watch for in terms of a ripe harvest in your community. For one thing, God seems to work among groups in bringing a ripening harvest. There have been reports that Vietnam boat people are coming to Christ in large numbers in nearly every country where shelter has been provided for them. During the initial months of massive layoffs in the automotive industry the harvest among unemployed auto workers in the Detroit area increased. Previously they were difficult to reach because high salaries provided them the ability to buy what they thought they needed for security.

Look across your town, city, or county for churches that are growing. Attempt to spot the areas from which they are drawing new people. If you have families living in those areas, they may be keys for your outreach ministry. What kinds of people are being won? Make a list of adjectives descriptive of the new converts. They may be of one nationality, socio-economic level, similar home background (example: all from rural Arkansas), race, or age. Keep searching until you find that common bond. One church discovered a high percentage of single-parent families whose children were deprived of love and discipline. These families were almost totally unchurched. The pastor developed a special weekday evangelistic and recreational ministry for the children. This program has resulted in children being won to Christ and opportunities for witness to parents.

Once you have identified the kinds of people who seem to be most open to the Gospel just now, the Chamber of Commerce or library can probably assist you with information on the total number of that kind of people in your county. You'll then have some idea of how many yet need to be reached. What if you don't find such a distinctive group? Don't lose heart. Most Christians are living in counties where over one-third of the people are totally unchurched and over one-half do not know Christ personally. Keep concentrating on those non-Christian friends, relatives, and neighbors. The Lord of the harvest will honor your faithful witness for Him.

10

Sin City

Beware – Satan is alive today.

Acts 18:1-6

¹After this, Paul left Athens and went to Corinth. ²There he met a Jew named Aquila, a native of Pontus, who had recently come from Italy with his wife, Priscilla, because Claudius had ordered all the Jews to leave Rome. Paul went to see them, ³and because he was a tentmaker as they were, he stayed and worked with them. ⁴Every Sabbath he reasoned in the synagogue, trying to persuade Jews and Greeks.

⁵When Silas and Timothy came from Macedonia, Paul devoted himself exclusively to preaching, testifying to the Jews that Jesus was the Christ. ⁶But when the Jews opposed Paul and became abusive, he shook out his clothes in protest and said to them, "Your blood be on your own heads! I am clear of my responsibility. From now on I will go to the Gentiles."

1 Corinthians 5:9-11

⁹I have written you in my letter not to associate with sexually immoral people—¹⁰not at all meaning the people of this world who are immoral, or the greedy and swindlers, or idolaters. In that case you would have to leave this world. ¹¹But now I am writing that you must not associate with anyone who calls himself a brother but is sexually immoral or greedy, an idolater or a slanderer, a drunkard or a swindler. With such a man do not even eat.

Deadwood, South Dakota. That name sounds familiar. Oh, yes, now I remember. We had a flat tire right in the middle of Deadwood on a trip west. It's a little town of about 2,500 just north of Rapid City and a few miles east of the Wyoming border. What brought it to mind was a news article regarding Deadwood's running battle with the state. South Dakota has a law making prostitution illegal. But Deadwood has no ordinance against it; in fact, Deadwood's main claim to fame for over 100 years is the four prostitution houses operating on the north edge of town. Every year or so the town hires new lawyers to work on its case. Loss of the four businesses would put thirty girls out of business and cut down significantly on the tourist trade the town enjoys. The people in Deadwood seem to think prostitution is a legitimate business. The owner/manager of one of the houses has been interviewed on national TV.

If you've read what Romans 1 says about the downhill path mankind has been on ever since the original sin, the situation in Deadwood doesn't surprise you. Your community may have its own brand of legalized prostitution or related businesses: massage parlors, adult bookstores, swinging singles bars. Whether the issue is immorality, crime, drugs, or any of the other ills affecting our society, sin is still alive and well in this world now ruled by Satan. The Book of Revelation says that the great enemy of mankind will be loosed for a little season just before Christ returns, and even a casual glance at what is happening in our society brings the conclusion that he's loose now.

Historians tell us that the things leading to the fall of the world's last great empire, Rome, are present again today on a worldwide scope. In every age there have been places that have fit the description. The city of Corinth in the first century was one of those places. Paul visited this city on his second missionary tour. Corinth was on the isthmus of southern Greece, about fifty miles west of Athens. It was a well-known Mediterranean seaport and an important commercial city. North-to-south caravans passed through. Sea traffic from east to west unloaded and carted cargo across the four-mile isthmus to save days of shipping time. A lot of people from all parts of the Roman world passed through Corinth. Like many seaports of the day, it was a center of immorality. Like Deadwood, South Dakota prostitution was big business. The religion of Corinth centered around worship of Aphrodite, the goddess of love. A thousand prostitute priestesses served at her temple. "He lives like a Corinthian" became a widely used expression to describe an immoral person, and to call a woman a Corinthian meant she was a prostitute.

As historians describe the lifestyle and conditions in the United States in the last quarter of the twentieth century, they seem to be borrowing a page from the history of first-century Corinth. The similarities are unmistakable. Some are actually calling this the post-Christian era, meaning Christianity has had its day and now has passed. They suggest by this that it is time for some other philosophy to come on the scene. Christians know that is not true. History is not one meaningless drama after another being played out on the world's stage. It is moving onward to a grand climax when Christ returns to restore His world to its original beauty and splendor. Therefore this is *not* a post-Christian era, except in the sense that society is secularized. The day for effective Gospel ministry ends only when the trumpet sounds and Christ breaks through the clouds. Until then the Gospel of the kingdom must be preached as a witness.

Yes, our society is much like that of first-century Corinth. If God could work in Corinth's filth and immorality to win men and women to Himself—and He did—then let us confidently expect Him to do likewise in our twentieth-century Corinthian-like world. Only those who have not kept in touch with God's great plan will doubt that the Gospel is still "the power of God for the salvation for everyone who believes" (Rom. 1:16).

Bible Base

Read Acts 18:1-16. (1 Corinthians will give additional background.) Verses 1-4 reveal one of the ways Paul made contacts in a strange city. Though his calling was primarily as a missionary to the Gentiles, he followed the pattern of first going to the local synagogue to discuss Jesus, the Messiah, with the Jews. What a pleasant surprise it must have been for him to meet a Christian Jewish couple there in Corinth. Most Jews were closed to Paul's Gospel presentation, but a group called God-fearers was present in synagogue meetings, and they were usually the first converts as a result of Paul's teaching. God-fearers were Gentiles who had accepted the teaching of the true God. They could not participate in some of the Jewish worship rites but were allowed to be present for the teaching from the Scriptures. Paul's powerful presentation of faith in Jesus Christ as the way to acceptance by God was just the message God-fearers needed. It didn't require them to submit to Jewish ceremonial laws that were so foreign to their culture. Does your church have its ceremonial laws and traditions that may keep people from coming to Christ and growing in your fellowship? It is easy to add to the requirements of the Gospel: repent of sin and receive Jesus Christ by faith.

Paul's synagogue ministry was based on proclaiming Christ as Saviour and urging his listeners to respond by accepting

Christ as the promised Messiah. He wouldn't accept our common definition of witnessing: sharing Christ in the power of the Holy Spirit and leaving the results to God. Along with reasoning about the Scriptures, he realized the need to be God's instrument in pressing people to make a positive response. This is New Testament evangelism.

Verses 5-8 describe the result when resistant Jews continued to hear the Gospel presented. A God-fearer named Justus lived near the synagogue and made his home available to Paul. From here on Paul's ministry was mainly to Gentiles. But the ruler of the synagogue had been so impressed with Paul's teaching that he believed on Christ and joined the new Christian group along with his family. This ministry to Gentiles living in Corinth was quite effective. The letters of 1 and 2 Corinthians mention people of Corinth who believed. And think of all the people passing through who heard and carried the message back to their own villages. The converts were mostly slaves and pagans from the lower levels of society, though a few prominent Gentiles also believed: Erastus, the city treasurer; an influential man named Crispus, and a wealthy woman named Chloe. The example of Corinth makes clear that there is no difference: the Gospel can save rich and poor, slave and free, male and female.

Verses 9-11 give an indication of how important God felt the ministry in Corinth to be in His overall plan. Paul may have thought of moving on soon, but in a vision God told him to continue preaching. In many towns and cities, Paul stayed only a few weeks, but in response to the vision he spent eighteen months ministering in Corinth. He left a growing congregation.

People don't live in a vacuum, even people who are in vital union with Jesus Christ. Everyone is affected by culture, whether we like it or not. The Christian who does not have a TV is the exception, for instance. For years missionaries overseas have dealt with various cultures and developed ministries accordingly. The Gospel message does not change, but the way we present it and develop it must change from culture to culture. The same is true in your community. If my method of preaching and teaching the Gospel in the inner city is the same when I minister in extremely rural locations, the hearers in one place or the other will not perceive the Gospel as relevant to them. The Corinthians are good examples. Paul's message had to stress certain aspects of the Gospel that dealt with problems faced because of their culture.

Read 1 Corinthians 5:9-11. Recall the description of Corinthian culture. That is why Paul had to deal with such problems in the church as immorality, greed, idolatry, slander, drunkenness, and fraud. In fact, 1 Corinthians deals with at least fourteen church problems which grew out of the society in which these Christians lived.

Implication

It happened in South Carolina. The youth group of a coastal church spent several weeks discussing how they could share Christ with people from the pagan culture. They chose a tract for use as a witnessing tool and practiced how to share it conversationally. Finally the day came when they went to the beach to try witnessing for Christ. Their counselor offered prayer, and then they fanned out by twos. In mid-afternoon they got together to compare notes. All of them had been able to witness to at least one person, and the total number who heard the Gospel was sixty-three. Ten teens and two adults had prayed to receive Christ, and the team members had given each one a card with the church name and service times listed. It was a pretty happy group. Not every person they spoke with had listened, but it was exciting to know that so many would allow them to share what Christ was doing in them and how they made Him their Saviour.

On Sunday morning the youth group gathered in their usual seats about halfway forward on the right in the auditorium. Just as the choir was marching in, the lead soprano's eyes opened wide with surprise. A stranger was coming up the aisle to sit with the teens. He was barefoot and wore a

T-shirt and cut-off jeans, and he greeted the teens loudly when he reached their pew. Didn't he know he was expected to wear a suit and shoes to church and keep quiet during the service?

No, he didn't know that. Over the next few weeks the church found out that this new convert knew very little of the other things Christians were supposed to know and do. You see, he had never been in a church before, except for a wedding. The teens and their counselor befriended him and encouraged him, but the rest of the congregation remained aloof. It looked as if he never would be accepted by the body. Then the youth counselor hit on an idea. On Sunday nights the pastor gave opportunity for testimonies during the song service. Jeff was invited to be present Sunday night. When testimony time came, the counselor suggested to Jeff that he share how he had found Christ. For the next ten minutes that congregation alternated between hilarious laughter and tears running down cheeks as Jeff described the emptiness of his life and now the joy and peace he had since the teens introduced him to his best friend, Jesus.

That did it. The service ended right there, and everybody flocked to Jeff to shake his hand, give him a hug, and thank him for sharing. As they got to know him in Christ, the marks of his culture were much less important. By the way, that was three years ago. He now wears shoes, slacks, and a nice sport shirt to church.

I hope you get the point. When a person receives Christ, the new creature in Christ becomes a reality. But Paul reminds us that the new Christian is like a baby; he'll have to crawl awhile before he learns how to walk and run and become spiritually mature. That's a good description of the Christian life—becoming spiritually mature, more like Christ every day. Because new converts are not spiritually mature, we have to exercise patience with them. Perhaps most recent additions to your church were children who grew up in your church or Christians transferring from other churches. They had a background of Christianity; they knew some of the things Christians expect from other Christians in terms of conduct and what God expects of them in terms of conduct. As you and your church begin reaching people for Christ from our pagan society, they may not have that foundation.

A friend of mine works in a city mission. When a down-and-outer receives Christ, he takes that man out witnessing with him the next day. It was a shock for me as I accompanied him and Sam the day after Sam's conversion. We stopped as Sam recognized two old friends. He shared what had happened to him through meeting Christ the night before. The testimony was laced with a lot of four-letter words and concluded with, "Christ has made me feel so damn good I can hardly stand it!" Three months later Sam and the mission director came to speak at our men's fellowship. I held my breath when Sam began to testify. But it was different: three months into the Christian life had affected his speech. The four-letter words were gone. Sam was growing in Christ.

A church that is expanding by reaching new families for Christ will experience problems. Our society is non-Christian just as the first-century society was non-Christian. But that is a problem you can deal with. Most of Paul's letters were written to counsel congregations regarding the difficulties they were experiencing as their old cultures and lifestyles clashed with the radical lifestyles of people who were growing into the image and stature of Jesus Christ. The only alternative to having some of these problems is to close the fellowship to any new people. Some churches that I am acquainted with have done just that. Sad to say, they are no longer in existence.

Application

The problems of the Corinthian church are typical of ours today. Identifying them will help us find solutions. Think about your church; then list its problems on the right side of the page. See if Paul's principles stated to the church at Corinth will help you resolve some of the problems that your church faces.

The problems in Corinth	The problems in my church
Quarrels and divisions 1 Cor. 1:10-17	
Poor stewardship 1 Cor. 4:1-5	
Pride 1 Cor. 4:6-21	
Sexual immorality 1 Cor. 5; 6:12-20	
Improper use of gifts 1 Cor. 11—14	

Churches increase in membership by one or more of three methods. The first is called *biological growth,* meaning new members who are children of existing church members. The second is *transfer growth,* which happens when somebody who is already a Christian transfers a membership to your church from some other church. The last is *conversion growth,* meaning persons who are won to Christ from outside present church families and are baptized and received into membership. A church that relies on biological growth dies a slow death, particularly now when families are having fewer children. Transfer growth may increase the size of your church membership but does not increase the number of people in Christ's church. You have just rearranged the same number of people on the playing field. The only way your church can advance Christ's kingdom is to pray for, plan for, and work for an increasing number of new members through conversion—people from totally unchurched families.

Think about the members added to your church over the past three years. What kinds of growth do they represent? Put their names in these columns. Discuss this with others so you don't overlook any new members.

Biological growth (existing families)	Transfer growth (already Christians)	Conversion growth (unchurched families)

To talk about reaching out to families who are totally unchurched can be frightening and threatening. We tend to think it is impossible. But God worked through faithful witnesses in corrupt Corinth. He has not changed over the years. His Gospel has not changed, and His power is just as great. It is up to us. From the vantage point of seeing how God worked in the past nineteen centuries, we should have no doubt that He will use us in the ripe harvest of our day. We know in advance that there will be problems. Our population in the under-forty age bracket is the first modern generation to grow up without a significant emphasis on biblical standards in the home and school. God renews our minds when we become Christians, so let's use those minds to design some ways of minimizing the problems of bringing former pagans into the church.

Here are some thought-starters concerning how other churches have successfully discipled people from unchurched homes:

1. Twelve-week classes for new converts to help them discover what Christ expects of His followers in terms of living standards, service, and ways of growing in grace.

2. Discussion sessions on Sunday nights to help older members understand the background of new Christians and

how to relate to them.

3. Monthly prayer/share groups made up of two mature Christian couples and one or two new Christians.

You have an important part in building Christ's kingdom. How will you answer these questions?

Am I spiritually prepared to fulfill my part in building the kingdom?

Is there any unconfessed sin in my life that I should deal with now?

Have I discovered and developed my spiritual gifts?

What is my responsibility in making disciples?

11

Decisions or disciples

More Christians should become *active* members of
the church.

Acts 11:19-21

[19]Now those who had been scattered by the persecution in connection with Stephen traveled as far as Phoenicia, Cyprus, and Antioch, telling the message only to Jews. [20]Some of them, however, men from Cyprus and Cyrene, went to Antioch and began to speak to Greeks also, telling them the Good News about the Lord Jesus. [21]The Lord's hand was with them, and a great number of people believed and turned to the Lord.

Acts 13:1-3

[1]In the church at Antioch there were prophets and teachers: Barnabas, Simeon called Niger, Lucius of Cyrene, Manaen (who had been brought up with Herod the tetrarch), and Saul. [2]While they were worshiping the Lord and fasting, the Holy Spirit said, "Set apart for Me Barnabas and Saul for the work to which I have called them." [3]So after they had fasted and prayed, they placed their hands on them and sent them off.

One of my seminary courses required research on the effectiveness of mass evangelism efforts. For my project I chose the "Here's Life America" campaign of Campus Crusade for Christ. After studying reports on "Here's Life" campaigns in about a dozen American cities, I listed three positive aspects:

1. Someone was doing something in a big way to communicate a positive message about Jesus Christ.

2. Church members were being trained and involved for follow-up of persons who prayed to receive Christ through the campaign.

3. The Gospel was getting high visibility. Probably no other group has put on such a first-class, high-powered media blitz for Christ. The "I Found It" message was on TV, radio, in the papers, and on bumper stickers.

The stated goal of the campaign was to blanket America with the Gospel and see many people saved. The first part of the goal was accomplished. However, my study indicated that, while thousands of people prayed to receive Christ as a result of *Here's Life,* only 3 percent of those making decisions ended up on the membership rolls of a church. And apparently 42 percent of *those* were already members of a church before the campaign. Let's not give Campus Crusade a black eye over this; they were willing to try something big for Christ. As the program goes on, they are revising and improving so that more of those who respond will be brought into the fold of a local church. Babe Ruth struck out three times for every home run he hit, and whether it is Campus Crusade or your church, you can expect to strike out at times. That's not sinful. Not attempting something for God is where sin comes in.

Christians talk about *decisions*. Do you know that word does not appear in the New Testament in relation to evangelism? However, the word *disciples* appears at least 260 times and in each case refers to new people being reached for Christ. Church reports show that decisions for Christ are being made in many congregations. Yet denominational manuals show a net membership loss over the previous three years. We have a high mortality rate between those who make decisions for Christ and those who ultimately become active members of the church. Should it be that way?

Bible Base

Read Acts 11:19-21. Following Stephen's death, things got pretty hot for the Christians in Jerusalem. They had the commission to make disciples of all nations, but they sat on it. It had been pretty comfortable there in the Jerusalem fellowship. But when Christians began upsetting the Jewish religion and tradition and interfering with Rome's influence, persecution began. Jewish Christians fanned out across the Roman world. To begin with, they followed the pattern used in Jerusalem: go to the synagogue and reason with the Jews and God-fearing Gentiles, and use key passages from the Old Testament Scriptures to show Jesus as Messiah.

Syrian Antioch was considered the capital of the eastern part of the Roman Empire. It was the eastern terminus of the great road that led into the heart of Turkey. People from many nations passed through Antioch. According to verses 20 and 21, several Christians broke the pattern of witnessing only in the synagogue and began sharing Christ with Gentiles as well. They were able to bridge over to these Greeks because they were also non-Jerusalem natives. The island of Cyprus or Cyrene, the Greek colony in North Africa, was their home. While Jesus as Messiah was the emphasis with Jews because of the prominence of this theme in the Old Testament, Gentiles did not have that background. What would be the meaningful way to introduce Christ to them? Beginning with the witness here in Antioch, the theme of Jesus as Lord becomes a part of the message. Gentiles could identify with that.

Antioch marks the turning point in the spread of Christianity in several ways. Here developed the first broad evangelism of non-Jews. This city became the first real missionary-sending center. Paul made it his base. Verse 26 says the believers were first called Christians here. When Gentiles had the opportunity of hearing about Christ the Lord without all the trappings of Jewish tradition, they understood and responded in great numbers.

Acts 13:1-3 gives another glimpse of this Gentile church at Antioch. The leadership represented quite a cultural mix. Barnabas was a Jew from Cyprus; Simeon, surnamed Niger or "black," suggests an African origin; Lucius was North African; Manaen was a foster brother of Herod Antipas, and Paul was a Jew. God brought a significant missionary crew to this cosmopolitan city, men who could relate to the various backgrounds of the converts. I'd like to have been there in Antioch, I think. Those were exciting days. It had taken ten years from the time Christians first arrived in the city after the Jerusalem persecution until they began sharing Christ with the Gentiles. But you can sense the rapid-fire spread of the Gospel. Those people were ready to hear and receive. The five teachers helped nurture the new converts so they would not slip back into their old life.

When their task was fulfilled, verse 3 shows the Spirit calling two of them, Paul and Barnabas, for still another mission. The Antioch Christians had a final worship service with them and blessed them as the first missionary journey of Paul began. Later verses report that this church gave financial support to Paul and Barnabas, and these men came back here when the tour was over to share results with the believers. That missionary pattern is followed today.

Implication

Jerusalem was the center of Christian ministry in the first 12 chapters of Acts, while the Gospel was preached primarily to the Jews. Syrian Antioch becomes the center for the last half of the book, as the Gospel is preached far and wide to men of every race and nationality. The two scenes we've looked at in Antioch have important implications for our church. Here, as in most places Paul visited, there was intensive instruction given to new converts. Follow him on those three missionary tours reported in Acts 13—21. Note the care given those who responded to the message. Did God send out His servants to get decisions, or to make disciples? The answer is quite clear.

Getting decisions for Christ creates a sense of movement in your church. It brings a warm glow to my heart whenever I see someone kneeling at the altar to receive Christ. But something is wrong when, after five or six years, the attendance remains the same. Recent studies indicate a mortality rate of 75 percent among new converts. Think of it: Only 25 out of every 100 who receive Christ actually become active members of a church and become involved in making disciples. Some churches are helpless to do anything about this. A Stone Mountain, Georgia congregation is a good example. If they had been able to keep all the converts they reported over the past ten years, the church would be three or four times its present size. But Stone Mountain happens to be near Metro Atlanta, where families live for an average of 13 months and then move elsewhere. Thank God this fact has not discouraged that church. They have sharpened their methods so that when a person comes to Christ through their ministry, he or she is immediately involved in training for Christian growth. They know that person may move in six months, and their prayer is that they can lay a strong enough foundation so the convert will remain true to Christ and seek church membership in the new location.

Your church probably isn't in such a mobile area. Nevertheless, the responsibility to involve new Christians in spiritual maturing is just as great. Getting decisions creates a sense of movement; making disciples brings real expansion to the church. An earlier chapter pointed out that in most counties in the U.S.A., at least 30 percent of the people are totally unchurched, and 50 percent or more do not know Christ as Saviour. The figures nationally are overwhelming: At least 100 million people are totally unchurched, and another 50 million who have their names on a church membership list are not in a personal relationship with Christ. Your opportunities for making disciples are nearly unlimited.

Application

What is your church's philosophy of outreach evangelism? One way to determine this is to list what the church does with and for a new convert. When I was a teenager my Sunday School teacher, my pastor, and one of the deacons dealt with me nearly every week until I made a public confession of faith in Christ. Then I had one meeting with the deacon, was baptized, and that was it. The only time I received a letter or call was when I missed Sunday School at least three weeks in a row. For a time I wished I had not made my decision so soon. The church didn't tell me I was to be on my own after that. I mustn't leave the wrong impression. The church family still cared for me, and I had many friends. But it was as though my walk down the aisle to receive Christ was the climax. Somehow after that, I was to gain instant maturity and perfection along with the instant pardon of sins and reception into the family of God. The last two things I was sure I did get. The maturity and perfection are still in process, thirty-six years later.

Churches who have adopted the philosophy of making disciples can be distinguished by the postnatal care they give to new Christians. They not only have spiritual obstetrics, but they also practice spiritual pediatrics. Paul and the other men in Acts 13:1 were acting in the discipling role, teaching the converts how to grow strong in their newly found faith.

In recent months I've made a list of some methods churches are using to make disciples as they help new Christians grow in the faith:

1. *New Christian classes.* These are usually held during the Sunday School hour for six-twelve weeks. Often the pastor or a deacon serves as leader. Subjects covered should be assurance of salvation, meaning of church membership, how to pray, how to study the Bible, how to witness, the doctrines of the church, something of the church structure and goals. To begin with, this might be offered once a year, then stepped up as the rate of new disciples increases. All who have come into the church since the previous class sessions should be expected to attend the current series.

2. *Support system.* Each new Christian is assigned to a church family who becomes his or her sponsors for the first year. Sponsors sit with the convert during services and meetings, make introductions to other church families, have a monthly social time with the convert and family, and make visits in the home when the person is sick or absent from worship. It really helps.

3. *Church organizations.* Every new disciple should be assigned to a Sunday School class, an appropriate fellowship group such as men, women, or youth, and placed on some service or outreach committee.

4. *Christian service.* Within six months of becoming a Christian the person is given instruction in spiritual gifts and guided to discover his or her gifts. Then, opportunities are provided for those gifts to be used. Pastors find this very helpful in getting new Christians into a pattern of spiritual growth.

5. *Monthly home Bible study* or prayer/share groups. These combine new and more mature Christians. The new Christians gain wisdom from the older Christians, and the older Christians catch some of the enthusiasm of the new ones.

Put a check in the margin beside those above that are

being used by your church.

Pastor William Batson has found the H.E.L.P.E.R. Evangelism program effective in nurturing Christians. The acrostic, H.E.L.P.E.R., stands for How to Equip Lay People to Evangelize Regularly. Pastor Batson says, "It is aimed at helping the pastor and laymen discover the important how-tos in developing a lifestyle of total evangelism in their church. Evangelism is more than just leading persons into a vital relationship with God through Jesus Christ. It is a lifestyle that ministers to the total needs of mankind. . . ." By involving new Christians in meaningful evangelism, he observes rapid spiritual development in their lives. The Lord is blessing. New converts are being trained and involved in reaching others. The cycle continues, and the church is enjoying a constant flow of new people into the fellowship.

Observe successful churches in your area. What principles are they applying to bring growth? Usually it will be related to the formula: find a need and fill it; find a hurt and heal it. That will apply to finding and reaching unchurched people, and it will work in developing ministries to hold them once you reach them. New converts are not as willing to be spectators in the church as some of us may be. Capitalize on their enthusiasm and drive. If you can keep them on target for Christ, your new Christians will have many contacts with unsaved people. Pray for them, train them, and encourage them to touch their spheres of influence. A constant flow of new converts is the best advertising your church can have.

What will work for your church? A book can only provide suggested resources and general ideas. You and other concerned members of your church will be able to discern the methods that best fit your congregation and your community. Pray for God to give you an open mind. Then discuss with others what they think it would take to reach some of the people on your responsibility list. You'll want to continually update that list, as you think of other friends, neighbors, and relatives who are not yet Christians. If this sounds like a lot of work, it is. But it will be worth all the effort you put into it when you begin seeing some of those you are responsible for becoming disciples of Jesus Christ.

For the past twenty-five years, Lyle Schaller, author and consultant, has been involved in church research. One of his stock questions to church members is, "Why are you a member of this parish rather than some other?" Between two-thirds and three-fourths of the people give friendship or kinship ties as the reason. In rapidly expanding congregations, up to seven-eighths of recent new members attended at the invitation of a friend or relative. Friendship ties are mentioned more often than kinship ties. Expansion in your church can begin without going out and bringing in new people totally unlike the present members. Most of your friends are from your basic social and economic level. You can be most effective with them, and they will feel at home in your church with you. Think about it, pray about it, then do something about it.

12

I can reach my world!

Evangelism is . . . reaching out to those around you.

An evangelical church commissioned an artist to paint a canvas to be displayed in the foyer that would depict the theme of evangelism. After sketching out several possibilities, the man painted a picture of a storm at sea. Fierce black clouds filled the sky spelling out imminent disaster. Caught in the flash of a bolt of lightning was a small boat being dashed by some breakers in the torrential waves. The pounding ocean was taking its toll, and the boat was disintegrating. Several sailors were in the water struggling to survive, crying desperately for help. There was only one possibility of hope. In the foreground, a large rock protruded out of the sea. And there, holding on with both hands, was one seaman.

When completed, the painting stirred your emotions. The tempestuous sea symbolized man's hopeless condition. The Rock of Ages properly symbolized the only way of salvation, the shelter in the time of storm. But as he compared his painting with Scripture, the artist realized that he had not captured the true picture of evangelism.

Out came another canvas, and he painted a second scene, much like the first. It was the same storm—the ominous clouds, the lightning, the brutal waves. The same boat was disintegrating in the breakers, with the crew frantically trying to find some safety. The same rock was there in the foreground. But that is where the change came. Now the seaman is holding on to the rock with just one hand, while, with the other, he is reaching out to lift up a sinking friend.

That is New Testament evangelism—one who has just been saved from sure death, reaching out a hand to help a fellow struggler with the offer of life. Without the outstretched hand there is no hope, and there is no Gospel. The Good News is that Jesus Christ has overcome the powers of Satan and sin and offers to save us from the same enemy. A Bible teacher who assisted me in my early Christian experience put it like this, "Evangelism is like one beggar telling another beggar where to find bread." You and I have found the Bread of Life, and we know He satisfies. All around us are people who have not yet made life's greatest discovery. We are called to be God's messengers. He has put at our disposal all kinds of opportunities and has given spiritual gifts to each of us, so that our tool kits will be sufficient to aid us in any situation of service for Him.

The purpose of this book has been to expand your vision to see new possibilities for outreach through your church, to help you learn from methods used by early churches and Christians, and to introduce principles and methods you might use to help make your congregation a more powerful force in reaching the lost of your community. "Make disciples" was the Master's command; we dare not busy ourselves with other tasks and leave this one undone. The leadership of our churches must be committed to the goal of making disciples and to assisting their churches in accomplishing the task. That is where the real action must be, in your church and the other communities of believers in our nation.

You are a key person in the success of this work in your church. The task is awesome, but like Paul, you can tackle the job with zeal and say, "I thank Christ Jesus our Lord, who has given me strength" (1 Tim. 1:12).

Where do you go from here? You begin by developing a game plan for making disciples right where you are. This particular study is nearing completion. Its benefit to you will be determined by what you do with what you have learned and experienced. God will be pleased as you and others in your church make the effort to lay plans, bathe them in prayer, and then work those plans for His glory. Remember, methods don't work. You work, using appropriate methods. Then you can be assured that God will give the increase.

This process is working in many places. In the spring of 1984, Jim Beede came to a church in Ballwin, Missouri, west of St. Louis. This was Jim's first pastorate. He found a very small but loyal congregation and a good church building. While another large church is just a block away, Jim and the congregation felt there were many people yet to be reached. That handful of people developed two strategies for initial penetration of the community. A well-planned, thoroughly advertised Vacation Bible School was held in June. Forty children attended, most from unchurched homes. This opened doors to new families, and almost immediately two new families were in attendance every Sunday.

The second strategy involved community visitation. Some churches might feel the pastoral staff is paid to do that; let them knock on doors. But those lay people saw that the community penetration must be thorough and completed soon. The deacons and elders themselves agreed to go out as visiting teams every other Sunday afternoon. As they prayed together and considered the lifestyle of the community, it was decided that just a community religious survey was not going to be adequate. The age of most of the families indicated that a straightforward witness would be accepted. And that's what's happening. Twice a month these men are knocking on doors, sharing with the residents their testimony of what Jesus Christ means to them. Then each family is asked two questions: 1. "Do you know Christ personally?" 2. "Are you active in a church?" For any families that answer no to either question, the pastor does a follow-up call during the week. Ballwin, Missouri is discovering that Christians have a personal relationship with a living Lord. And more and more of those residents are giving Pastor Beede the privilege of a return visit to bring them to Christ and into His church. New faces on Sunday morning are standard now. The whitening harvest is being reaped, disciples are being made.

My interview with Pastor Beede revealed that the congregation took eight steps in reaching out to their unsaved neighbors. These steps may help you in planning in your church.

1. *Find the needs.* During the visitation, the teams look for social, economic, and spiritual needs the church might be able to meet to establish a beachhead.

2. *Establish specific goals.* Dizzy Dean said, "If you ain't got no goal, you sure ain't gonna hit it." It sounded spiritual for the church to say that it would reach the lost in their town, but how can you tackle that and measure results? No church can be all things to all people. The board decided on a specific portion of the city that they should claim for a harvest field. They then began to decide what should be the special ministry of their church in view of the community needs they found.

3. *Continuing prayer.* At each step, the entire congregation goes to prayer for God's guidance. Before each afternoon of visiting, prayer is offered, and some people remain in prayer while the elders and deacons are calling.

4. *Establish new programs.* After evaluating the goals and praying for guidance, the church determines what specific programs will help accomplish the goal. Since there are many families with elementary and junior high children, it appears that a recreation program will become one of the outreach tools.

5. *Appoint leaders.* Because their active membership was just thirty-two at the beginning, they knew one another well enough to sense who was best gifted for the various programs.

6. *Provide needed equipment.* To develop a recreation program, they must clear brush at the rear of the property, get some softballs and bats, volleyballs and net, and so on. A possible day-care program will require some dividers for the

fellowship hall, sleeping mats, and a variety of toys. A bulging junior class will need a larger classroom, more chairs, and a new record player.

7. *Budget for the program.* Once the above six steps have been completed, you can put a price tag on each outreach program. A church wanting to expand will find that God will provide the additional funds necessary. Members may give more in view of the effective ministries. New people attending will increase offerings. You will be willing to cut back in some other areas in order to give financial priority to making disciples.

8. *Evaluate the results.* The best looking plan is only a piece of paper. It has no value unless it accomplishes the goal. Every expenditure of your church budget might need to be examined in the light of its ability to help meet the priority goal of evangelism.

Think again about the fact that 60-90 percent of new church members say they first attended a church because a friend or relative invited them. That sounds like a key for outreach in your church. You have a significant influence and association with a group of non-Christian people, perhaps as many as six to ten. Before discounting that figure, think through some of those people.

The Great Commission flies over the church as a banner, an all-consuming cause. This book has shown you possible ways of improving the response of your church to the command to disciple your world. There will be doubters galore when you begin talking about bold new plans for extending the kingdom and increasing the size of the congregation. This is normal. The church in every age has had doubters. But when a core of people are willing to venture out in faith and pay the price for a thriving church, God joins them and blesses their plans and efforts. In spite of heavy resistance, David Livingstone went to Africa to take the Gospel to an unreached nation. William Carey went to India, even after strong discouragement from the church, and India saw a new day of evangelism. Orville Harvey moved to Princeton, West

Virginia with the vision of starting a church. There were many doubters and even friends who called it an impossible task, since he had to work in a steel mill all day and drive an hour each way. The church continues to grow and recently purchased additional land for future expansion.

Five years from now, what will be written about the increase in your church because of people willing to venture out in faith to do God's will?

Several times the subject of meeting people's needs has been presented. This is a way of making contact and starting the evangelism cycle. How do you find those needs? One indicator of a person being receptive to change is his or her lifestyle. Two physicians in the West discovered that people were more susceptible to heart attacks at times of personal or family transition. During times of transition, people are also more open to a lifestyle change. It is not difficult to spot these transition times. The physicians even charted forty-one of them showing their relative impact. The death of a spouse is the most traumatic event a person faces, followed by divorce, marital separation, and personal injury or illness. A birth, a son or daughter getting married, a change in employment or residence, vacations, and even a speeding ticket have some temporary bearing on a person's openness to change. We need to stick with some of our friends and kinfolk closely enough so that we can observe when these transition times are occurring. As you look at your community, there are also some ways of discovering transitions in lives. The newspaper can be a great aid. Check announcements of births, marriages, deaths, and human interest events in families who are in your target area.

A few years ago our nation was shaken with the Watergate scandal. As one participant after the other was tried and imprisoned, those terms marked tremendous transition times in their lives. Thank God that there were Christians who sensed this and began witnessing to them. Senator Howard Hughes saw this as an opportunity to share Christ with Charles Colson, and after several meetings, Colson received

Christ. At least four others implicated in Watergate eventually come to Christ.

This book has presented a wide variety of ingredients that go into the program of a congregation that desires to grow. They include the pastoral leadership, the kind of people already in the church, the burden to proclaim the message, wide use of laypersons, effectively leading new members to responsible church membership, and the financial comitment to growth. This list is not exhaustive. How do you know the right mix of ingredients for your church? You keep trying.

When it comes to cooking, my wife is an experimenter. She gets a basic idea from a recipe, then comes up with her own. Little by little she adds flour, milk, shortening, spices, checking consistency and flavor regularly. At last she has the right mix, and it goes in the oven for forty-five minutes. The result may not have a name, but it usually tastes very good.

You and your fellow church members need to do the same thing. Get general ideas from this book and others listed in the resource section. Make a list of all your resources. Then begin combining ingredients. You'll know you have the right mix when the result is new faces in morning worship, a growing flow of people through the baptistry and into church membership, and indications that the new members are reaching out to their friends with the Gospel.

* * *

To Think About
There are six things that go into the profile of a healthy church. This list may help you in organizing your thinking and making bold new plans for making disciples.

HEALTHY CHURCH PROFILE
1. *Know where your converts come from.* Identify which witnessing method is most effective for your community, whether the Sunday morning altar call reaches new converts, how many find Christ through evangelistic calls in the home,

and what Presence Evangelism methods are working best for you.

2. *Plan for results.* Have a written strategy for expansion with definite goals for the years, steps for reaching them, and persons who are responsible for each part of the plan.

3. *Train people for evangelism.* The rule of thumb that 10 percent of the members have the gift of evangelism keeps you seeking out members with this gift, providing training for them, and then using them to follow up with families who have been cultivated by others.

4. *Incorporate new members into the church.* New members are immediately tied in through a new member class, Sunday School class, and fellowship group. They receive instruction in how to witness to friends, relatives, and associates.

5. *Use many channels of ministry.* Don't put all your eggs in one basket, but have enough outreach programs so there is a place for every member to be involved.

6. *Specialize in what works best for you.* Don't try to do everything at the same time. Experiment to discover what methods and programs bring results and which ones don't. Then concentrate on those that work. This is good stewardship of time, people, and money. At times you will start some new methods. And you'll regularly phase out those that are no longer effective.

The concluding paragraph of chapter 1 suggested that by the end of this book you would have many ideas to aid you in developing strategies for New Testament evangelism through your church. I pray this goal has been accomplished.

NOTES

Chapter One
1. Donald McGavran, *Understanding Church Growth* (Grand Rapids, Mich.: Eerdmans, 1970), p. 46.
2. Charles F. Pfeiffer and Everett F. Harrison, *The Wycliffe Bible Commentary* (Chicago, Ill.: Moody Press, 1962), pp. 1107-1108.
3. J. Edwin Orr, *The Fervent Prayer* (Chicago, Ill.: Moody Press, 1974), chap. 1.

Chapter Two
1. Earl F. Palmer, *Salvation by Surprise* (Waco, Texas: Word, Inc., 1975), p. 143.
2. Leslie B. Flynn, *Nineteen Gifts of the Spirit* (Wheaton, Ill.: Victor Books, 1974), p. 88.

Chapter Three
1. James F. Engel and H. Wilbert Norton, *What's Gone Wrong with the Harvest?* (Grand Rapids, Mich.: Zondervan, 1975), p. 143.

Chapter Four
1. Elton Trueblood, *The Company of the Committed* (New York: Harper and Row, 1961), p. 45.
2. Ray Stedman, *Body Life* (Glendale, Calif.: Regal Books, 1972), p. 73.
3. Lloyd Perry and Edward Lias, *A Manual of Pastoral Problems and Procedures* (Grand Rapids, Mich.: Baker Book House, 1962), p. iv.

Chapter Six
1. Ray Stedman, *Birth of the Body* (Santa Ana, Calif.: Vision House, 1974), pp. 56-57.

Chapter Seven
1. J.B. Phillips, *The Young Church in Action* (New York:

MacMillan Co., 1955), p. vii.

2. Adrian Shepard, "Harvest Now! Our Thrust in Evangelism," in *Advent Christian Witness* (Charlotte, N.C.: Advent Christian General Conference, May 1980). Monthly magazine.

Chapter Eight

1. William Steuart McBirnie, *The Search for the Early Church* (Wheaton, Ill.: Tyndale House, 1978), p. 122.
2. Dean R. Hoge and David A. Roozen, *Church Growth and Decline, 1950 to 1978* (New York: The Pilgrim Press, 1979), chap. 1.
3. "Christianity Today—Gallup Poll," *Christianity Today* (Christianity Today, Inc., Carol Stream, Ill.) Reported in semi-monthly issues beginning December 21, 1979.

Chapter Nine

1. McGavran, *Understanding Church Growth,* p. 33.

APPENDIX **A**
SHARING THE BASICS

As we mature in Christian living, we learn that there is more to the Gospel than we saw at the moment of conversion. Gradually, it dawns on us that Christ's salvation is too wonderful for words; that its full dimensions defy comprehension.

But as these wonders unfold, we often become tongue-tied in sharing the offer of salvation with those outside. We don't want to leave out any important details; so when a person seems ready to trust Christ, we are tempted to hand him a textbook on systematic theology. If we aren't careful, we may try to give a crash course on everything from the nature of man to the fine points of eschatology.

If someone said, "You have two minutes to tell me how to find salvation," could you beat the clock?

Here is one brief statement of Gospel basics. Committing these ideas and verses to memory will help you in dealing with someone who is ready to become a Christian.

Step 1. *God loves you and wants you to experience life—abundant and eternal.*

"I am come that they might have life, and that they might have it more abundantly" (John 10:10, KJV).

Step 2. *But most people do not have this experience. Why? Man chose to disobey God and go his own, willful way. Man still makes this choice today. Result: separation from God. Without Him there is no life.*

"For all have sinned, and come short of the glory of God" (Rom. 3:23, KJV).

Step 3. *Jesus Christ is the only answer to man's separation from God. When He died on the cross and rose from the dead, He paid the penalty for our sin. He has made it possible for men to receive abundant, eternal life.*

"For there is one God and one Mediator between God and men, the man Christ Jesus" (1 Tim. 2:5). "Jesus said . . . 'I am the way, and the truth, and the life; no one comes to the Father, but by Me'" (John 14:6, RSV).

Step 4. *We must trust Jesus Christ and receive Him by personal invitation.*

"Here I am! I stand at the door and knock. If anyone hears My voice and opens the door, I will go in and eat with him, and he with Me" (Rev. 3:20). Is there any good reason why you cannot receive Jesus Christ right now?

Prayer: I do want to follow You, Jesus. I regret the time I have spent running in the wrong direction, the people I've hurt, the way I've hurt myself. I'm sorry for all that. Forgive me. I know You can and will forgive me because You died for me. I do believe that. Thank You, Lord. I also believe that You rose again from the dead, that You are alive now, and that I can know You. And I want to know You. So here I am—for better or worse. Amen.

APPENDIX *B*
THREE-P EVANGELISM PLANNING CHART

The process: (See chapter 7 for description of three-P Evangelism)

1. List One-P, Two-P, and Three-P activities tried during the past three years. On a scale of 1-5 (1 = poor; 5 = excellent), how successful were they?
2. What methods might we use to accomplish the purpose of each type of evangelism?
3. What will be required in terms of money, personnel, and materials for each method? When might we carry this out?

One-P:
PRESENCE
The church makes its presence felt in the community. Result: People are helped in some way.

Two-P:
PROCLAMATION
The Gospel is proclaimed so people understand what a decision for Christ involves. Result: People hear, understand, and may make a decision to receive Christ.

Three-P:
PERSUASION
New Christians are incorporated into the church and become responsible, reproducing members. Result: People are in active fellowship with other Christians and involved in making disciples.

While this book is designed for the reader's personal enjoyment and profit, it is also intended for group study. A Leader's Guide with Victor Multiuse Transparency Masters is available from your local bookstore or from the publisher.